# Supply Chain Management:

# Business Operations in India

# Supply Chain Management: Business Operations in India

Edited by
Jan Stentoft Arlbjørn
Henning de Haas
Mads Bruun Ingstrup
Dennis van Liempd

University Press of Southern Denmark
2010

© The authors and University Press of Southern Denmark
Printed by Grafisk Produktion Odense ApS
Cover design: Ulla Arlbjørn
ISBN: 978 87 7674 484 7

University of Southern Denmark Press
Campusvej 55
5230 Odense M
Denmark
www.universitypress.dk

# Table of Content

Preface ................................................................................................ 11

Introduction ........................................................................................ 11

Four Themes ....................................................................................... 11

The Students ...................................................................................... 13

Organizing the Trip ........................................................................... 13

Travel Plan ......................................................................................... 13

Thank You .......................................................................................... 14

**Chapter 1: Prologue - Why Study Business in India?** ............... 19

Introduction ....................................................................................... 19

General Information About India ................................................... 20

Economic Development in India ..................................................... 24

Economic Drivers of the Indian Economy ............................ 25

Economic Development in Karnataka and Tamil Nadu ....... 27

Trends Impacting Global Supply Chain Management ................. 27

General Trends ........................................................................... 28

Product Related Issues ....................................................... 28

Relationship Based Issues .................................................. 29

Technology Related Issues ................................................. 29

Globalization Related Issues .............................................. 30

Competition Related Issues ................................................ 30

Recap on Reasons for Studying Business in India ...................... 31

**Chapter 2: Business Process Outsourcing** ............................... 33

Introduction ....................................................................................... 33

Literature Review .............................................................................. 34

Outsourcing ................................................................................ 34

Off-shoring .................................................................................. 35

Business Process Outsourcing ............................................... 35

Theoretical Perspectives on Outsourcing .................................... 37

The Make-or-Buy Decision .................................................................. 38

Transaction-Cost Theory ............................................................... 39

Competence-Based View ................................................................ 40

Relational View ............................................................................... 41

A Make-or-Buy Decision Model for Business Process Outsourcing .. 41

The Location Decision ..................................................................... 43

Dunning's Eclectic Paradigm ....................................................... 43

Location Decision Model for Business Process Outsourcing ............. 44

Research Questions .......................................................................... 47

Methodology ..................................................................................... 48

Empirical Studies .............................................................................. 49

Empirical Overview ....................................................................... 60

Conclusion ......................................................................................... 60

Implications .................................................................................... 62

**Chapter 3: Business Clusters and Localization in Southern India** ....... 63

Introduction ...................................................................................... 63

Literature Review ............................................................................. 65

What is a Cluster? ......................................................................... 65

The Competitive Advantage of Clusters ...................................... 66

Main Characteristics of a Competitive Cluster ................................ 67

The Cluster's Effect on Its Participants ......................................... 68

Access to Specialized Inputs and Employees ............................. 69

Access to Information .................................................................... 69

Complementing Each Other in the Cluster ................................. 70

Access to Institutions and Public Goods .................................... 71

Incentives and Performance Measurement ................................. 71

Summary of Porter's Cluster Theory ........................................... 72

Sources of Locational Competitive Advantage ............................... 72

The Role of Government ................................................................ 74

Location Specific Advantages ......................................................... 75

Infrastructure .................................................................................................. 75

Access to Raw Materials and Semi-Manufactured Goods ........................ 76

Access to Skilled Labor ............................................................................... 77

Macro-Economic Factors ............................................................................ 77

Reflection on Porter and Dunning's Theories ......................................... 77

Methodology .................................................................................................. 78

Empirical Findings ........................................................................................ 79

Company Descriptions .............................................................................. 80

Company A .............................................................................................. 80

Company B .............................................................................................. 80

Company C .............................................................................................. 80

Company D .............................................................................................. 81

Expected and Experienced Advantages/Disadvantages ......................... 81

Company A .............................................................................................. 81

Company B .............................................................................................. 82

Company C .............................................................................................. 83

Company D .............................................................................................. 85

Discussion ...................................................................................................... 86

Cluster Location Matrix ........................................................................... 86

Defining the Axes ..................................................................................... 86

Defining Quadrants and Placing Company A-D .................................. 87

Conclusion ..................................................................................................... 90

**Chapter 4: Relationship Management** ............................................... 93

Introduction .................................................................................................. 93

Methodology .................................................................................................. 94

Literature Review ......................................................................................... 96

Indian Culture ........................................................................................... 96

Environmental Factors ............................................................................. 97

Consideration of Company Specific Variables ...................................... 98

Inside-Out vs. Outside-In ...................................................................... 99

Portfolio vs. Integrated ............................................................... 99

Discrete vs. Embedded................................................................ 99

Relationship Management in Practice .......................................... 99

Key Account Supplier Management.......................................... 100

Implementation of Relational Strategies ................................. 102

The Overall Framework for Analysis ....................................... 103

Analysis.......................................................................................... 105

Cultural Differences...................................................................... 105

Dimensions to Deal with in Relation to Indian Suppliers.................. 106

The Relationship Between India and the West From a Cultural
Perspective .................................................................................. 109

Benefits for Indian Companies.................................................. 109

Benefits for Western Companies.............................................. 110

Environmental Factors................................................................... 110

India and the Global Recession................................................ 111

Democracy................................................................................ 111

Communication........................................................................ 112

Domestic Market or Export?.................................................... 112

Consideration of Company Specific Variables ............................. 113

Inside-Out vs. Outside-In ........................................................ 113

Portfolio vs. Integrated ............................................................ 113

Discrete vs. Embedded............................................................. 113

Relationship Management in Practice .......................................... 114

Why Focus on Key Suppliers?.................................................. 114

Implementation of Relational Behavior Strategies ............................. 114

Key Account Management........................................................ 115

Conclusion .................................................................................... 117

Culture............................................................................................ 117

Environment................................................................................... 117

Company Specific Variables ......................................................... 118

Relationship Management ..................................................................... 119

**Chapter 5: Corporate Social Responsibility** ............................... 121

Introduction ........................................................................................ 121

India .................................................................................................... 122

Methodology ....................................................................................... 123

Theoretical CSR Definition ............................................................... 125

UN Global Compact ......................................................................... 126

Empirical Data: CSR Paradoxes ........................................................ 127

Paradox 1: Karma vs. Caste ............................................................ 128

Karma ........................................................................................... 128

Caste .............................................................................................. 129

Paradox 2: Philanthropy vs. Embedded in Strategy .................... 133

Paradox 3: Global vs. Local Adaptation ....................................... 136

Paradox 4: Official CSR-Policy vs. Multitude of Programs ........ 139

Paradox 5: Own Workforce vs. Outside Agency Employees ....... 142

Paradox 6: Bribery vs. Anti-Bribery ............................................. 145

Conclusion ......................................................................................... 147

Summary ....................................................................................... 147

Managerial Recommendations .................................................... 148

Perspective .................................................................................... 149

**Chapter 6: Epilogue - Learning and Reflection** ......................... 151

Introduction ...................................................................................... 151

Most Impressive Experiences ........................................................... 152

Application of Relevant Theories and Methods ............................. 153

Improved Competencies Through Group Work ............................. 154

Better Understanding of Indian Culture ......................................... 155

The Most Important Points of Cultural Learning .......................... 156

Conclusion ......................................................................................... 157

Outsourcing and Off-Shoring ...................................................... 157

Business Clusters and Localization .............................................. 158

Relationship Management ........................................................................ 159

Corporate Social Responsibility ............................................................ 160

**List of References** ...................................................................................... 161

**Index** .......................................................................................................... 167

**About the Editors** .................................................................................... 169

# PREFACE

## Introduction

This book is titled "Supply Chain Management: Business Operations in India", and contains assignments from Danish management students related to a study trip to India in the fall of 2009. The study trip was a Master Level elective called "International Field Studies" for a M.Sc. in Business Administration, at the Department of Entrepreneurship and Relationship Management, University of Southern Denmark, Kolding.

The general purpose of the field study elective was to develop the students' skills in applying general theories as well as specific methodologies and analysis tools to actual business problem areas. Furthermore, the purpose was also to let students acquire practical experience with respect to the technical and social competencies, which international field studies require. The aim of the course was therefore to train students in conducting all phases and facets within a smaller field study, including the initial preparatory desk research, the practical organization of the field work and the subsequent follow-up analyses and research reports.

## Four Themes

In the present context, this field study aimed to achieve general knowledge about doing business in India, and to outline challenges from a Western perspective that are relevant in an Indian business and cultural environment. More specifically, the students examined the following four topic areas:

1. Outsourcing and off-shoring
2. Business clusters and localization
3. Relationship management
4. Corporate Social Responsibility (CSR)

Many large and small companies have relocated their labor-intensive production and/or administrative processes overseas to traditionally low-wage countries such as India. The liberal reforms implemented by the Indian government in past decades, has made Business Process Outsourcing

11

(BPO) the fastest growing industry in India. This makes outsourcing and off-shoring an interesting theme for further investigation.

Clustering and localization are becoming more important on the business agenda in order for companies to benefit from different location-specific advantages. The benefits of being located in a business cluster e.g. increased cooperation and access to high value resources are vital drivers for business development. However, localization can be many things and companies engage in business clusters differently according to their needs and characteristics. In an Indian context, this poses a series of both opportunities and challenges, which companies have to relate to.

Companies are often interacting with a large number of suppliers, customers and other stakeholders. However, it is not cost free to engage in close business relationships. Many resources are being spent on their development and maintenance. Therefore, companies need to differentiate their business relationship practices depending on the concrete situation. This motivates the need to dig deeper into relationship management in an Indian context.

Finally, CSR is included as a study object, because doing business in a global environment can cause ethical and moral value challenges that multinational companies have to address. Companies have to satisfy demands by external stakeholders in the form of e.g. suppliers, customers, Non-Governmental Organization's (NGO's), (local) communities and authorities, and internal stakeholders such as managers and employees. But CSR, ethics and morals do not necessarily have the same meaning in India as in the West. Doing business in India thus poses some specific CSR challenges, which are worthwhile to examine further.

All topic areas are viewed from a global Supply Chain Management (SCM) perspective. Following this, the students have reviewed and discussed theories and collected data related to the four topic areas mentioned above. Their assignments have been written in English in order to be able to report back to the companies visited. Furthermore, a publisher has been engaged in publishing their assignments. This has been decided based on a belief that publication will improve the final output of the students' learning process. The result is the present book.

## The Students

The students were comprised of two groups: M.Sc. in Management and Leadership students and M.Sc. in International Business Development students. The M.Sc. line in Management and Leadership is structured around two central competency areas. The management part provides knowledge and tools for solving problems regarding SCM, operations management and management accounting. The leadership part ensures an understanding of and competence in solving problems within leadership, organizational changes and strategy development. The M.Sc. line in International Business Development has three central competence areas: 1) a fundamental competence within organization and management, 2) a line-specific competence in business development and teamwork and 3) a line-specific competence in international business relationships. The four groups were composed of students from both M.Sc. lines. The names of the specific students are listed on the front page of the theme-specific chapters.

## Organizing the Trip

First of all, it has to be mentioned that the students have planned this field study trip by themselves. The planning period was about eight months long, consisting of e.g. identifying, contacting and setting up appointments with companies, conducting fundraising, providing communication about the study trip to stakeholders, and organizing flights and hotels, transportation to and from companies, and sight-seeing trips. In order to solve these tasks, the students were organized into different working groups with representatives meeting in an overall steering group. The actual field study trip took place from the 24th of October to the 1st of November 2009.

## Travel Plan

The overall trip consisted of company visits in Bangalore and Chennai, South India. The field study trip started in Bangalore, where the *Trade Commission of Denmark* visited our hotel Monday morning and gave a general presentation on the business climate in India. Monday afternoon, three separate companies were visited. The relationship management and business cluster groups visited *Samrat Gems Impex,* which is an Indian textile-manufacturer who sub-supplies amongst others a large Danish textile company and large US retail chains. The CSR group visited the sales office of Danish pharmaceutical company *Lundbeck* for a presentation of their

CSR activities in India. Finally, the outsourcing and off-shoring group visited the Danish-owned relocation services firm *Santa Fe* regarding topics related to establishing and operating a third-party service facility.

On Tuesday morning, all four groups visited Danish bio-innovation company *Novozymes* which is located in the International Technical Park in Bangalore. This visit covered presentations related to all four study themes, and also included a visit to Novozymes's warehouse and re-packaging facility. After the visit, the group traveled by bus from Bangalore to Chennai – a ride of about seven hours. Wednesday was free for company visits and dedicated to sight-seeing instead.

On Thursday, each group visited two companies. Danish wind-mill manufacturer *Vestas* and Danish cement and mineral equipment and services provider *FLSmidth* were visited by the business cluster and CSR groups. These visits included presentations and guided-tours of the respective facilities. The relationship management group first visited Danish producer of mechanical and electronic products and controls *Danfoss*, a visit which beyond discussions on relationship management issues also included a guided-tour of the entire plant. In the afternoon, the relationship management group joined the outsourcing and off-shoring group in visiting American IT-services firm *UST Global*. Earlier that day, the outsourcing and off-shoring group had visited Scandinavian consultancy firm *Valcon* to get a perspective on best management practices related to their theme. Finally, on the last day (Friday) all four groups visited the Danish pump solution firm *Grundfos*. This visit also included a guided factory tour.

## Thank You

Many people have been involved in making this field study trip possible. We would therefore like to thank the people and organizations listed below for their generous support (time, knowledge and/or financial).

*Funding for the Trip*
Department of Entrepreneurship and Relationship Management, University of Southern Denmark, Kolding
Business Economics staff-student committee, University of Southern Denmark, Kolding
Ole Kirks Fond, Denmark
Fabrikant Mads Clausens Fond, Denmark

*Funding for the Book*
Toosbuys Fond (ECCO)
Cheminova A/S

*Companies That Have Been Visited*
We would like to give many thanks to all companies visited for their hospitality in opening their doors on their practices, perspectives and blueprints for the respective themes for this field study trip. Below are listed all persons that have made the visits valuable learning sessions:

*Trade Commission of Denmark*
Trade Councellor, Harish Muthanna
Trade Commissioner, Ricki Toftelund Larsen
Trainee, Kristian Bach Kolding

*Samrat Gems Impex PVT. Ltd.*
General Manager Anil Gosain
Manager-HR, Aravind K. Angadi

*Santa Fe*
Joint Managing Director, Diwakar Gupta
Vice President, Priya Kuttaiah

*Lundbeck*
Senior Marketing Manager, Janakiraman S.

*Novozymes*
Regional President, G. S. Krishnan
Regional Finance & IT Director, Uno Steffensen
Executive Assistant, Ranjit Narayanan

*Danfoss Industries Pvt Ltd*
Whole-time Director & President, K. Hariharan
Manager – Sales (HVACR), S.R. Gopinath
Manager – Production Planning & Logistics, S. Ramanadoss
Deputy Manager – Production, Rajeev Rajan

*UST Global*
Director, Ramakrishnan Narayanan
Director – Business Development, Satheesh Ananthasubramanian
Transition Manager, Srikanth Srinivasan
Manager – Human Resources, Remadevi Thottathil
Center Operations, Karkuzhali Shanmugam

*FLSmidth*
Managing Director & CEO, Anders Bech
Sr. Manager, Minerals – Plant Engineering, S. Ranganathan

*Vestas*
Deputy General Manager, Production & Supply Chain, P. Kumar
Sr. Manager – Corporate Communication, Madhu Kumar Boppana
Assistant Manager – Vendor Development (PBU), R. Satish Kumar

*Valcon*
CEO, Krishnan Naganathan

*Grundfos*
Managing Director, Ranganath N.K.
Business Director, B. Chandra Sekaran
GET – Marketing, H. Narendhran

*People with inspiration and technical support*
Louis Møllerfors, Piapium
Associate professor, Birgitte Norlyk, University of Southern Denmark for a
lesson on academic writing for the entire group

Last, we would like to give a special thanks to the students for a well-organized field study trip and for their pro-active learning attitude. The students have done a tremendous job by organizing company visits, booking hotels and flights and planning sight-seeing events. We certainly believe that this trip has given the students a learning experience technically, socially and culturally which will be useful for their future carriers. This book is the result of their collective effort, and has been their examination assignment. Therefore, the individual chapters' content and conclusions are the sole work of the students, and do not necessarily reflect the opinion of the editors.

Best regards and we hope you enjoy the book!

Kolding, April 2010

Jan Stentoft Arlbjørn
Ph.D., professor

Henning de Haas
Ph.D., post.doc.

Dennis van Liempd
Ph.D., assistant professor

Mads Bruun Ingstrup
Ph.D.-student

# CHAPTER 1

## Prologue: Why Study Business in India?

*Jan Stentoft Arlbjørn, Henning de Haas, Mads Bruun Ingstrup and Dennis van Liempd*

### Abstract

*For some years, India's economy (GDP) has been able to continue to grow by 4-8 percent per annum. Having a huge population with good language skills, a large domestic market, and continuous financial growth makes it interesting to investigate the climate for doing business in India in a Global Supply Chain Management context. Topics of interest are questions like - what are the actual cultural, social, and economic conditions, opportunities and challenges for doing business in India? How fast is India developing and how will competition from industrial development influence the cooperation with Danish companies? These are some of the questions that many companies are posing, when considering if and how to do business with India. The purpose of this prologue is to set the scene for discussing these questions in the context of Global Supply Chain Management.*

### Introduction

Except for the last 400-500 years, India has been a very rich and developed country for millennia. Since the 1990s, when the government started a number of economic reforms, India has been very well under way to be a leading economy again (Pagadala and Mulaik, 2009). India is a huge country: often people talk about India as one country, but it would be more appropriate to talk about India in the same way as e.g. about the USA or Europe, consisting of a number of smaller countries and states with different languages and dialects. It is important to understand this diversity when doing business in India.

India is a nation with a young population (a large part is below 15 years of age). Another interesting fact about India is that a great majority of the population is employed in agriculture even though this sector only contributes with one fifth to Indian GDP. At the same time, there is a large and growing middle class demanding the same lifestyle and opportunities as they see in the USA and Europe. This is driving a large domestic market for goods and services. A major driver for the growth in Indian GDP is a well-educated and motivated population, which to a large extent has good language skills. This contributes to the ease of doing business in India and the ease of foreign companies to settle in India.

The Indian government continuously initiates programmes for developing and expanding the business infrastructure. This is both the financial infrastructure, including tax rules and regulations, and the physical infrastructure – roads, airports etc. Some initiatives are based on Public Private Partnerships, where the government, together with private investors, provides highways and airports. However, projects and new ways of cooperating to build infrastructure are being hindered and slowed down, e.g. due to problems regarding bureaucracy and democratic protests in the local communities.

## General Information About India

*Bharatiya Ganarajya*, or the federal Republic of India, is the world's largest constitutional democracy, with at its head President Pratibha Patil (since 25 July 2007) and Prime Minister Manmohan Singh (since 22 May 2004; Government of India, 2010). The central government is located in North-India, in the capital city of New Delhi (15 million inhabitants). India has a bicameral Parliament (*Sansad*), consisting of the Council of States (*Rajya Sabha*; max. 250 members) and the People's Assembly (*Lok Sabha*; 545 seats). India's legal system is based on English common law, with judicial review of legislative acts, while the Supreme Court is the highest court in the country (Government of India, 2010).

### Geography

Like a giant wedge between the Arabian Sea and the Bay of Bengal, India is the 7th largest country in the world. With its 3.287.263 km$^2$ it is around 76 times larger than Denmark. Besides bordering Bangladesh, Bhutan, Burma, China, Nepal and Pakistan, India has 7000 km worth of coastline. For business purposes, it has to be remembered that India is 5.5 hours ahead of UTC (Government of India, 2010).

The country is divided into 28 states and 7 union territories[1], of which our study trip visited the capitals of the South Indian states of Karnataka (Bangalore; 7.2 million inhabitants) and Tamil Nadu (Chennai; 6.6 million). Climate-wise, Southern India has a tropical monsoon climate, with monsoons from late May to October. With respect to natural resources, India possesses the fourth-largest reserves of coal in the world. Furthermore, it has deposits of iron ore, manganese, mica, bauxite, titanium ore, chromite, natural gas, diamonds, petroleum, limestone, and arable land (48.83 percent) (CIA World Factbook, 2010).

When doing business in India, it should be remembered that some (localized) natural hazards exist, such as droughts, flash floods, as well as widespread and destructive flooding from monsoonal rains, severe thunderstorms, and earthquakes.

Current problem areas with respect to the environment are deforestation, soil erosion, overgrazing, desertification, air pollution from industrial effluents and vehicle emissions, water pollution from raw sewage and runoff of agricultural pesticides, tap water is not potable throughout the country, and the huge and growing population is overstraining natural resources (CIA World Factbook, 2010).

**History**

Indians are proud of their long history, which is one of the oldest in the world, at least going back to the Indus Valley civilization of the 3rd and 2nd millennium BC. Around 1500 B.C., Aryan tribes from the northwest infiltrated onto the Indian subcontinent and merged with the earlier Dravidian inhabitants, creating the classical Indian culture (Government of India, 2010). Dravidian culture remains strongest in the state of Tamil Nadu. The Mauryan Empire of the 4th and 3rd centuries B.C. united much

---

[1] *=territory. Andaman and Nicobar Islands*, Andhra Pradesh, Arunachal Pradesh, Assam, Bihar, Chandigarh*, Chhattisgarh, Dadra and Nagar Haveli*, Daman and Diu*, Delhi*, Goa, Gujarat, Haryana, Himachal Pradesh, Jammu and Kashmir, Jharkhand, Karnataka, Kerala, Lakshadweep*, Madhya Pradesh, Maharashtra, Manipur, Meghalaya, Mizoram, Nagaland, Orissa, Puducherry*, Punjab, Rajasthan, Sikkim, Tamil Nadu, Tripura, Uttar Pradesh, Uttarakhand, and West Bengal.

of South Asia, while the Indian Golden Age was ushered in by the Gupta dynasty (4th to 6th centuries A.D.). The Arabs started their incursions in the 8th century, while European traders and colonialists began their expansion in the late 15th century. By the 19th century, the British Empire controlled virtually all Indian lands politically (Government of India, 2010). Non-violent resistance to British colonialism led by Mohandas Gandhi and Jawaharlal Nehru brought independence in 1947. Sub-continental India, which originally included Pakistan and Bangladesh, was divided into the secular state of India and the smaller Muslim state of Pakistan. A third war between India and Pakistan in 1971 resulted in East Pakistan becoming Bangladesh (Government of India, 2010). Despite impressive gains in economic investment and output, India faces pressing problems such as significant overpopulation, environmental degradation, extensive poverty, and widespread corruption (CIA World Factbook, 2010).

## Population

According to the latest official census of 2001, India has a population of 1.027 billion, second only after China, which India is expected to surpass in 2030 (Government of India, 2010). Since the population grows at around 1.548 percent per year, unofficial estimates for July 2009 put the population number at 1.166 billion (CIA World Factbook, 2010). Compared to Europe, India has a very young population, as can be seen in Table 1.1, with a median age around 25 years.

Table 1.1: Indian Population by Age (2001 census)

| Age Group | Percentage |
|---|---|
| 0-14 yrs. | 31.1 % |
| 15-64 yrs. | 63.6 % |
| 65 + yrs. | 5.3 % |

Source: CIA World Factbook (2010)

29 percent of the total population lives in urban areas, while the annual rate of urbanization growth is 2.4 percent. 72 percent of the population is of Indian-Aryan descent, 25 percent of Dravidian descent, while 3 percent is of Mongoloid descent and others (CIA World Factbook, 2010).

The middle class is estimated at 300 million, and growing fast. Literacy rates (defines as age 15 and over who can read and write) are 61 percent for the total population (male: 73.4 percent; female: 47.8 percent) (2001 census).

The average school life expectancy is 10 years (male: 11 years; female: 9 years (2005; CIA World Factbook, 2010).

India is showing a growing gap in the male-female ratio, causing a shortage of marriable women. Life expectancy at birth is 69.89 years for the total population. With an adult prevalence rate of 0.3 percent (2007 est.), around 2.4 million people currently live with HIV/AIDS. India also has many major infectious diseases, with a high risk for food or waterborne diseases (bacterial diarrhea, hepatitis A and E, and typhoid fever), vector borne diseases (chikungunya, dengue fever, Japanese encephalitis, and malaria), animal contact disease (rabies), and water contact disease (leptospirosis) (CIA World Factbook, 2010).

## Language

There are 18 official languages in India, and more than 840 dialects (for most important languages, see Table 1.2). English can be considered a national language, because it is the most important language for national, political, and commercial communication. The quality of both spoken and written

*Table 1.2: Languages in India (2001 census)*

| Language | Percentage | Language | Percentage |
|----------|-----------|----------|-----------|
| Hindi | 41.0 % | Kannada | 3.7 % |
| Bengali | 8.1 % | Malayalam | 3.2 % |
| Telugu | 7.2 % | Oriya | 3.2 % |
| Marathi | 7.0 % | Punjabi | 2.8 % |
| Tamil | 5.9 % | Assamese | 1.3 % |
| Urdu | 5.0 % | Maithili | 1.2 % |
| Gujarati | 4.5 % | Other | 5.9 % |

Source: CIA World Factbook

English is therefore high in India, especially compared to countries like China.

## Religion and Caste

Within this multitude of people, cultures, and languages, there is one common element that pins down the national psyche: religion. Every day, devout practitioners worship at temples, mosques, churches, or their home shrines and altars. Hindus make up the majority as can be seen in Table 1.3.

*Table 1.3: Religion in India (2001 census)*

| Religion | Percentage |
|---|---|
| Hinduism | 80.5 % |
| Islam | 13.4 % |
| Christianity | 2.3 % |
| Sikh | 1.9 % |
| Other | 1.8 % |

Source: CIA World Factbook (2010)

The Hindu pantheon consists of around 330 million deities, with Vishnu, Shiva, and Ganesh among the most important ones. Religion-based communal conflict is unfortunately not uncommon, but much less noticeable in the south than in the north.

Although the caste system is not recognized in the constitution, castes are still very important in India, especially in the rural areas. Cast still influences both vocational and marriage prospects. The four main castes in India are:

- The Brahmin (priests and scholars)
- Kshatriyas (soldiers or administrators)
- Vaishya (merchants)
- Shudra (laborers).

Castes are further divided into thousands of *jati*, groups of 'families', or social communities, which are sometimes linked to occupation. Caste is the basic social structure of Hindu society, and living a moral life by fulfilling your duties is considered paramount. Beneath these four castes are the *Dalits* (formerly known as Untouchables), who hold menial jobs like cleaning and getting rid of corpses (Fuller, 2004).

## Economic Development in India

India is one of the four largest transition economies in the World, and the country has a remarkable track record in economic growth since the beginning of the 1990s. From the time when India got its independence in

1947, the country has gone from a centrally planned economy to a more international open market economy. Today, India is a member of both the G20 and the WTO. The economy has grown with more than 7 percent from the mid-1990s (Danish Ministry of Foreign Affairs, 2009), and this high growth results mainly from market reforms, huge inflows of foreign direct investment (FDI), rising foreign exchange reserves, an IT and real estate boom, and a prosperous capital market. India will become one of the world's largest economies by 2050 if it continues to grow at the current rate (Shiralashetti and Hugar, 2009). This impressive economic growth needs to be understood in a number of historic episodes, which date back to the British occupation.

During the occupation, the British government laid down a number of economic policies to enhance trading activities with foreign countries. Besides benefiting the British economy, these policies also led to large scale trading and the development of industries in India (Roy, 2007). After independence in 1947, five-year plans were introduced in order to estimate and project various economic policies. The first plan primarily aimed at developing the agricultural and industrial sector (Economy Watch, 2010). When Gandhi took office as prime minister, private participation was promoted, and foreign companies, specifically petroleum companies and banks were nationalized (Economy Watch, 2010). First in 1991, economic liberalization took speed and started the engine behind today's high economic growth in India.

## Economic Drivers of the Indian Economy

One of the policies following economic liberalization was the decision to open the Indian economy to foreign investments. Especially the Indian manufacturing and service sectors have benefitted from this decision, and in 2008 inward FDI flow grew with 446 percent, compared to 2005 (UNCTAD, 2009). On the other hand, outward FDI flow is only growing slowly indicating a lack of innovative power and ownership-advantages in the current state of the Indian economy.

Alongside foreign investments, all three sectors in the Indian economy, agriculture, manufacturing and services, have in different ways driven economic growth. As far as agriculture is concerned, India is the world's second-largest producer in volume of output (Economy Watch, 2010). Related industries to the agricultural sector have also supported the growth in the Indian economy by providing employment to a number of people in the forestry, fishing and logging industries. In 2005, the agricultural sector was employing 60 percent of the Indian labor force, but only contributing with 18.6 percent to GDP (Economy Watch, 2010). Since the 1950s, production volumes have increased due to various five-year plans, but these plans have not taken distribution of the final production into serious consideration. This means that even today large shares of the agricultural production go to waste due to lacking and obsolete supply chains.

In the manufacturing sector, India is the world's number 14 in volume of factory output (Economy Watch, 2010). Especially the gas, mining, electricity and quarrying industries are the main contributors in terms of jobs and economic growth. The service sector is the Indian economy's wonder kid, largely due to the amount of foreign investments from America and Europe during the 1990s and early 2000s. Large numbers of the labor force are occupied in the service sector, which in a ten year period between 1990 and 2000 grew with 7.5 percent (Economy Watch, 2010). Companies involved in IT development, call centers and business process outsourcing (BPO) are in particular frontrunners in the service sector. To illustrate the importance of the service sector, its contribution to GDP was more than 50 percent in 2007 compared to almost 30 percent in the manufacturing sector in the same period (Danish Ministry of Foreign Affairs, 2009).

Additional factors that have supported economic development in India are growing foreign exchange reserves and a prosperous capital market – but it is not all glamour and growth. India is facing hard economic times with an inflation rate of nearly 8 percent (OECD, 2008). Inflation is considered a threat to the economy, as increasing inflation puts an upward pressure on wages and prices. The rising costs of oil, food and resources needed for India's construction boom are also affecting budgets. Despite the wish to promote a balanced utilization of resources, unemployment is a problem in India (Bandara, 2005).

Perhaps the biggest economic threat is the degree of poverty. According to the government, in 2007 nearly 220.1 million people were living below the UN poverty line, and nearly 21.1 percent of the entire rural population and 15 percent of the urban population live in difficult physical and financial circumstances (Economy Watch, 2010). These parts of the population have not experienced the benefits connected to the economic growth. The government has both nationally and regionally a task to meet the poor's needs as well, as they are important in the up-coming phases of development in the country, both in order to maintain stability and to create a platform for future growth.

## Economic Development in Karnataka and Tamil Nadu

As seen in the general info section, India is an extremely large country with many differences across the nation including economic differences. During the field trip, we visited Bangalore in Karnataka and Chennai in Tamil Nadu. Both states are located in the southern part of India.

Karnataka, and especially Bangalore, is the home of the Indian IT sector, and primarily Bangalore has benefitted highly in terms of jobs and growth. GDP growth for the State of Karnataka was 7.2 percent in 2008, mainly due to the service sector (Government of Karnataka, 2009). In the following year, the service sector was contributing with 56 percent of the state's GDP as compared to 27 percent by the manufacturing sector and 17 percent by the agricultural sector. This trend of moving activities from agriculture to manufacturing and services can also be seen in the employment figures where employment in the agricultural sector has declined from 67.3 percent in 2000 to 58.4 percent in 2005. Employment in the manufacturing sector grew from 12.8 percent to 16.1 percent, while the service sector also registered an increase in employment from 19.9 percent to 25 percent, during the same period (Government of Karnataka, 2009).

The State of Tamil Nadu is one of the most industrialized states in India, and it attracts 9.12 percent of total FDI in the country, only surpassed by respectively Maharashtra and Delhi (The Hindu, 2009). Economic activity in the state is divided in the following way: Agriculture 21 percent, manufacturing 34 percent and services 45 percent (Tamil Nadu Online, 2009). The service sector is, like in Karnataka, the most important economic driver, but Tamil Nadu is moreover known for its heavy engineering, vehicle manufacturing, manufacturing of electrical goods and equipments and textiles. The textile industry alone contributes to 4 percent of the state GDP, and the textile cluster in Tirupur is the single largest exporter of garments in the whole country (Tamil Nadu Online, 2009).

## Trends Impacting Global Supply Chain Management

This section briefly discusses some global business trends within supply chain management (SCM). SCM is concerned with the transformation of demand information to physical deliveries of goods and services. It starts with end customer needs for goods and services which create demand for goods and services backwards in the supply chain and supply network. Ideally, SCM provides differentiated management of intra- and inter-organizational activities and processes with the purpose of fulfilling customer requirements by delivering goods and services from the point of origin to the point of consumption to the overall lowest costs at the right time and at the highest quality level (Arlbjørn, 2006). SCM has a concurrent focus on maximizing the twin objectives of increasing the top-line (turnover) through service improvements and improving the bottom-line through cost reductions.

**General Trends**

Companies today operate in an ever more turbulent business environment. Lately, the world is experiencing a financial down turn, putting pressure on cash flows and thereby also on key SCM elements, such as inventories, lead-times, operational efficiency etc. This all demands higher awareness and maybe a faster pace on changing and optimizing supply chain performance.

These challenges are pointing in a number of different directions though, leading to a need for prioritizing between different optimization efforts. Such challenges can be summarized in five headlines:

1. Product related issues
2. Relationship based issues
3. Technology related issues
4. Globalization related issues
5. Competition related issues

The following lists briefly give examples of possible challenges within these five subject areas.

**Product Related Issues**

- Product lifecycles are becoming shorter and shorter which increases the need for capabilities in phasing products in and out.
- Customers are demanding product variations: customers want unique products which puts pressure on a company's innovation processes.

28

- Individual needs can be met through modularized product design.
- Products are not only physical in nature, but may also contain value added services.
- Due to increased global awareness on environmental issues, return and recycling issues of products are becoming a high priority on management agendas.

## Relationship Based Issues

- Cooperation and relationship management are important concepts when dealing with supply chains and networks.
- The company's boundary is stretched into the extended enterprise with deep relations with certain customers, suppliers and even competitors.
- There is an increased need for knowledge transfers between companies.
- More specialized suppliers are used and organized in clusters and networks.
- As relations between customers and main suppliers are becoming closer the barriers for other suppliers are increasing.

## Technology Related Issues

- Rapid technological developments are providing companies with new tools to communicate and create traceability through global supply chains (such as Radio Frequency Identification and Global Positioning Systems).
- There is a growing focus on the possibilities for trading through e-solutions and there are already solid solutions ready for implementation.
- New technologies are used as a differentiation parameter which creates new possibilities regarding products and processes.
- New systems set new requirements for integration of the company's entire system platform.
- In spite of rapid technological developments, new systems cannot deliver better results than the quality of data they are being fed with (e.g. correct and complete master data).

## Globalization Related Issues

- Customers, suppliers, competitors and other industrial actors are doing business on a global scale – from local to global (some companies are even born global).
- Globalized supply chains are creating new challenges in business processes, coordination and operational issues of longer lead-times.
- Operations in globalized supply chains demand cultural and language skills.
- Globalized operations may lead to higher complexity and require excellent documentation management (master data management, drawings, bill-of-materials, certificates etc.).
- Long-distance relationships across many time-zones (capacity, inventory levels demand higher competency levels).

## Competition Related Issues

- There is a focus on core competencies; based on make-or-buy analyses, companies are off-shoring/outsourcing non-core areas such as production, inventory management, transportation, IT and administrative functions (often termed Business Process Outsourcing). This practice may also drain the company's innovation skills and demands new skills in organizing and managing inputs in innovation processes.
- Environmental consciousness is emerging as a competitive parameter which is closely related to issues concerning global warming and consumption of natural resources (e.g. use of recycled packaging, $CO_2$ minimized distribution, reduced pollution, carbon footprint).
- Corporate Social Responsibility issues are receiving more strategic awareness in companies (e.g. securing that suppliers are not underpaying their workers, are not offering dangerous working environments and are not employing child laborers).
- Time to market is a strong competitive parameter (i.e. the ability in realizing and marketing new product ideas fast).

- Innovations in supply chains in terms of technology, business processes and network structure (Arlbjørn and de Haas, 2009) are a source for competition in line with product and market innovations.

Besides the above lists of management issues, globalized supply chains are also becoming more vulnerable. The following (contradictory) factors have made supply chain operations more vulnerable:

- A focus on efficiency instead of effectiveness (inventory levels are reduced through Just-In-Time waves and information sharing replace inventories).
- Globalized supply chains (increased lead-times have led to buffer stocks in local markets that have the potential to be obsolete).
- Focused factories and centralized distribution (products are moving more; "parts tourism").
- Outsourcing (loss of experience and control).
- Reduced supplier base (increased dependency).

## Recap on Reasons for Studying Business in India

This chapter has outlined some major reasons why India is a hotspot for studying business and supply chain management. Major reasons for doing so can be as be summarized as I-N-D-I-A:

- Impact: India is a fast growing country with a huge impact on the world's economy (in terms of development of population and business activities).
- Next: India is the next generation outlet for business development.
- Development: The development of the Indian nation, which happens in different tempos (on a scale of poorness to richness), is both an opportunity and a challenge – will the nation break?
- Intelligence: With its many skilled workers, India may be characterized as the brains of the world, whereas China is the labor factory of the world.
- Attractive: India's attractiveness in terms of growing sales market is huge (more than one billion people have a kind of purchasing power).

# CHAPTER 2

# Business Process Outsourcing

*Jens Hansen, Kent Hansen, Henrik Hvam, Søren Hut, Karsten Johansen and Sandie Nielsen*

## Abstract

*This chapter identifies challenges and opportunities faced by firms outsourcing or off-shoring business processes to India. It examines the various theoretical factors affecting both the make-or-buy decision and the location decision. The empirical data collection was carried out in a field study in India visiting and interviewing six different firms. The main opportunities discovered in this study regard cost advantages, market attractiveness and a large, skilled workforce whereas the main challenges consist of cultural distance, lack of innovative capabilities and bureaucratic Indian authorities. These factors, in combination with the specific firm strategy, determine which approach to follow: outsourcing or off-shoring.*

## Introduction

Increased competition through globalization has forced firms around the world to examine their organizations and reconsider what their core competencies consist of. This has been necessary in order to reduce costs and/or increase quality for customers, so the company is able to survive in an increasingly competitive market.

One way of achieving competitiveness is through outsourcing. Outsourcing is often presented as an effective path to cost reductions. Furthermore, studies indicate that short-term cost savings continue to be a predominant reason for both off-shore and domestic outsourcing (Corbett, 2005, Doig et al., 2001). Outsourcing allows firms to focus on their core competencies by buying products and services that are peripheral, from external suppliers, who may well be able to deliver these products or services cheaper and at better quality. Peripheral activities are defined as "all activities away from the firms core-competencies" (Monzka et al., 1998, p.

213) and core-competencies can be defined as *"a skill, process or resource that distinguishes a firm and makes it unique compared to other firms"* (Monzka et al., 1998, p. 213).

However, outsourcing has several implications beyond immediate price reduction. Outsourcing affects day-to-day management, performance, as well as the corporate strategy. Therefore decisions about outsourcing clearly affect a firm's cost structures, but may also affect the long-term competitive situation and alter the nature of risks that the firm must manage. This suggests that there is much more to outsourcing than simple cost reductions. Outsourcing creates both new opportunities and often unrecognized hazards which may limit a firm's prospects. The long-term costs of these unanticipated consequences can greatly overshadow the potential cost savings. Thus careful consideration should be given to outsourcing decisions including all of the potential long-term consequences (Ellram et al., 2008). Regarding outsourcing, there is much focus on developing countries such as India. This is due to the fact that India is a country in rapid growth with a variety of interesting aspects to consider when thinking about outsourcing. India's characteristics have made the country a very attractive place for outsourcing business processes. The focus of this chapter will therefore be on Business Process Outsourcing (BPO) in the context of India and the different aspects of this subject.

## Literature Review

In order to specify the exact meaning of central terms used in this chapter, a number of definitions will be outlined to clarify the topic *Business Process Outsourcing (BPO).*

### Outsourcing

The overall topic of this chapter is BPO, but in order to understand this term a basic definition of outsourcing will be helpful. Outsourcing is defined by Rushton and Walker (2007, p. 4) as *"...the strategic use of external specialized service providers to execute and manage activities or functions that are normally seen as non-core to the business"*. This definition assumes partly that the use of external suppliers is strategic and partly that these activities are of a peripheral type. This presents outsourcing as a thorough strategic decision whereas Pyndt and Petersen (2006, p. 11) define outsourcing in a broader sense: *"outsourcing denotes the activities where companies let an external and independent supplier perform the task in question"*. The only condition in the latter definition is that the activity is

34

performed by an external supplier in order to be characterized as outsourcing. This broad definition gives a clear reference and foundation for other terms of this topic. Furthermore, it seems to be widely accepted in the outsourcing literature (Ellram et al., 2008 and Hätönen, 2009) for which reason this latter definition will be the reference in the remainder of this chapter.

## Off-shoring

Off-shoring is often confused with outsourcing, even though fundamental differences cause different strategic implications. For this reason a clear definition of off-shoring is equally necessary. According to Pyndt and Petersen (2006, p. 12) off-shoring can be defined as "...activities in foreign locations. These activities may be performed in-house (off-shoring) or by sub-suppliers (off-shore outsourcing)". This definition characterizes all activities performed in foreign locations as off-shoring. This makes it possible to distinguish between off-shoring and off-shore outsourcing. Despite the differences between these two, many of the same considerations are relevant in both cases.

## Business Process Outsourcing

As mentioned before, the topic of this chapter is BPO which can be seen as a specific part of outsourcing in general. To define BPO it is important to understand the nature of a business process. Cooper et al. (1997) define business processes as "the activities that produce a specific output of a value to the customer". Thereby, business processes can be seen as a structured, measured set of activities designed to produce a specific output for a particular customer or market. BPO deals with the outsourcing of this particular type of activities and Mehta et al. (2006, p. 323) define BPO as "transferring the operational ownership of one or more of the firm's business processes to an external provider that, in turn, manages the processes according to some predefined metrics". This categorizes BPO according to the type of activity being outsourced. Examples of business processes in this context are: finance, accounting, legal services, marketing, customer care, human resources, sales, administration, billing, payroll, claims processing, product support etc. (Graf and Mudambi, 2005). Business processes can be divided into three types of services: 1) Front-office processing, 2) Middle-office processing, and 3) Back-office processing. This classification thus distinguishes the different types of activities by how directly they interact with the customer (Mehta et al., 2006).

Another classification system of business processes is based on the complexity of the service provided. Here, a *discrete* BPO activity refers to a single-process where the supplier is responsible for only one process. In a *comprehensive* BPO activity, the supplier undertakes multiple business processes within a single support area and in *multi-domain* BPO activities, which are more complex, the supplier supports the client's functions across multiple support groups (Mehta et al., 2006). These classifications are illustrated in Figure 2.1. Examples of each type of activity and degree of complexity are given in the boxes on the right side of the figure. One should however bear in mind that several of these examples can be characterized differently, depending on the way these are carried out. The classification of the examples in this figure however provides the most obvious and rational characterization of the individual examples.

*Figure 2.1: Classification of BPO*

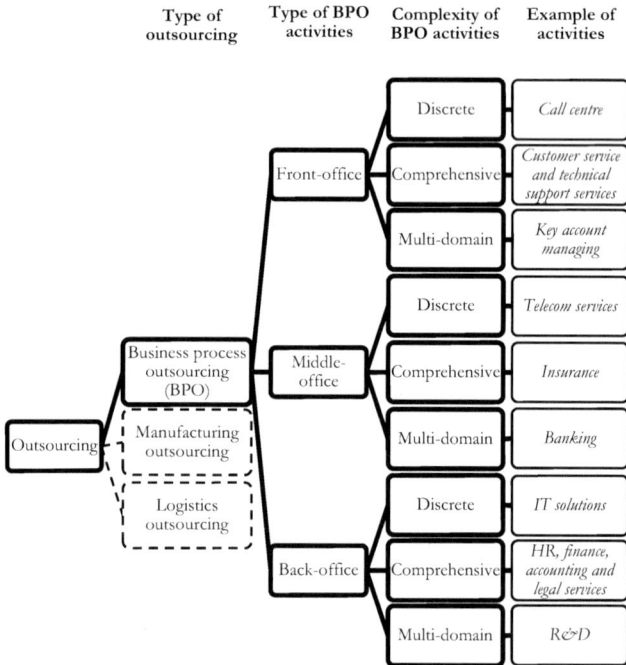

Source: Own compilation

To be characterized as BPO, the outsourced activity must be a business process, which in this chapter is seen as synonymous with a service activity, distinguishing it from manufacturing and logistics processes, as illustrated in Figure 2.1. The reason behind this assumption is that BPO can be viewed as a client buying a service from an external supplier. Hence, business processes in this chapter do not include processes within manufacturing and logistics.

*Table 2.1: Definitions*

|  | **In-House (Make)** | **External Supplier (Buy)** |
|---|---|---|
| **Domestic Location** | In-house operations | Domestic outsourcing |
| **Foreign Location** | Off-shoring | Off-shore outsourcing |

Source: Own compilation, inspired by Pyndt and Pedersen (2006, p. 11)

The concepts discussed above are illustrated in Table 2.1, where BPO can both take the form of domestic outsourcing and off-shore outsourcing.

## Theoretical Perspectives on Outsourcing

This paragraph presents some theoretical insights into what needs to be considered in the outsourcing decision. It will focus on two parts of the outsourcing decision, respectively; the make-or-buy decision and the location decision. These are illustrated in Figure 2.2 which will be the guideline for the structure of this paragraph. Figure 2.2 suggests that the make-or-buy and location decision are two separate decisions that need to be addressed when considering outsourcing. Even when the firm decides to perform an activity in-house, a location decision could be relevant following an off-shoring strategy illustrated by the dotted line. Therefore many similar factors should be taken into account when considering off-shoring or off-shore outsourcing. Furthermore, it can be seen that the location and the business partner selection decisions are closely related. Therefore, the choice of location cannot be isolated from the choice of partner as they are two interrelated processes (Hätönen, 2009). The theoretical perspective will focus on discussing which factors are determinants for the make-or-buy decision and the location decision respectively.

*Figure 2.2: The Outsourcing Decision Process*

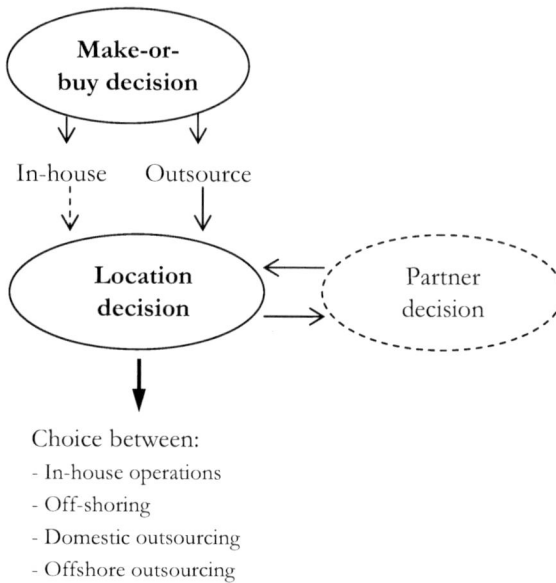

Choice between:
- In-house operations
- Off-shoring
- Domestic outsourcing
- Offshore outsourcing

Source: Own compilation inspired by Graf and Mudambi (2005, p. 255) and Hätönen (2009, p. 64)

## The Make-or-Buy Decision

Choosing products or services that can be advantageously obtained externally as opposed to produced internally is known as the make-or-buy decision. Make-or-buy is by Heizer and Render (2009, p. 154) defined as:

> *"The choice between producing a component or a service and purchasing it from an outside source". This implies that the make-or-buy decision is a decision on whether a firm should produce or purchase. This is critical, because it affects the level of costs, delivery schedules and quality.*

Therefore, the make-or-buy decision is an essential subject in relation to outsourcing. The make-or-buy decision can be based on the following two questions (Chopra and Meindl, 2007, p. 418):

- Will the other party increase supply chain surplus relative to performing the activity in house?
- To what extent do risks grow upon outsourcing?

38

Supply chain surplus is in this case the total revenue that all supply chain participants, including the customer, get to share. When conditions are at their optimum, supply chain surplus increases without significantly increasing risks. The surplus increases either when the value for the customer increases or when a decrease in total costs occurs. Total-cost reduction occurs when the other party effectively is able to aggregate assets or flows to a higher level than the firm itself. These assets or flows can for example be an aggregation of capacity, inventory, transport, warehousing or information.

In evaluating the make-or-buy decision, firms have to consider the risks in using an external supplier. First of all, it is important that the firm does not lose control over the process so the process will be inferior. Furthermore, the cost of coordination is often underestimated, especially when firms outsource and buy products or services from several other suppliers (Chopra and Meindl, 2007, pp. 418-430).

According to Mehta et al. (2006) there are three approaches to the make-or-buy decision, as illustrated in Figure 2.3: 1) The transaction-cost view 2) The competence-based view, and 3) The relational view.

*Figure 2.3: Three Views on the Make-or-Buy Decision*

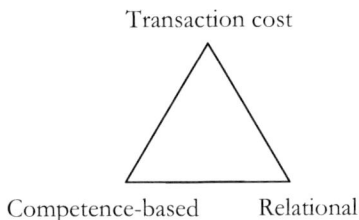

Transaction cost

Competence-based          Relational

Source: Own construction inspired by Mehta et al. (2006, p. 327).

## Transaction-Cost Theory

One view on the make-or-buy decision is based on transaction-cost theory. It discusses the choice between market (buy) and hierarchy (make) and the factors affecting this decision. The theory focuses on the costs of outsourcing, i.e. the cost caused by transactions in the market. Coase (1937) identifies transaction costs as costs that arise when purchasing through the market (making a transaction) instead of undertaking the process within the hierarchy. According to Williamson (1981, p. 552) a transaction can be defined as something that arises "when a good or service is transferred across a technologically separable interface". Thus, a transaction can be said to take place when a transfer is made beyond the boundaries of the firm.

Transactions can further be divided into three dimensions (Metha et al., 2006): 1) Frequency of transactions, 2) Uncertainty, and 3) Degree of asset specificity. These are the three determinants of transaction costs. Williamson (1981) developed Coase's view further by localizing the sources of transaction costs in human nature. Human characteristics such as bounded rationality and opportunism are argued to be the cause of these transaction costs or frictions. Opportunism is defined as an agent seeking self-interest with guile. This refers to an agent being dishonest and misleading for his own gain, which can cause firms to fear that the other party will misuse the relationship and thereby cause an increase in transaction costs. Consequently, the need for planning and monitoring activities in the market, e.g. through formal contracts, is increased. Besides uncertainty, asset specificity can also cause substantial risks which arise through partner-specific investments. This results in increased dependence on a specific partner, resulting in an increased risk of a hold-up situation.

The focus of transaction cost theory in the make-or-buy decision is on assessing transaction costs compared to the cost of making the product or service within the hierarchy. This decision determines whether a firm should outsource a given activity or not. Thus, a firm will perform an activity in-house as long as production/management costs are less than the transaction costs.

## Competence-Based View

The competence-based perspective is based on the nature of the firm's resources and capabilities. According to this approach, a firm should only outsource activities that are not core competences (Mehta et al., 2006). Thereby, it is implied that a firm should only perform activities internally that are regarded as core competences (Dong-Hoon Yang et al., 2007). Hence, in contrast to the transaction-cost view, the competence-based view focuses on the type of activity in question, not solely on costs. Ramachandran and Voleti (2004) present some activities as partly core thereby suggesting that there is a continuum between the two extremes of core and non-core activities. Ramachandran and Voleti (2004) suggest in this context that partly core activities should be medium outsourced. By this they mean that an external supplier can perform the activity, but the firm should maintain internal control of the process through some kind of partnership.

40

According to this view, it is clear that the type of activity is essential when considering the make-or-buy decision. It is argued that core activities of the firm should be kept in-house in order to sustain core competences through continuous learning. However, it would be reasonable to outsource activities that can be characterized as peripheral. Regarding peripherals, it is often the case that other parties effectively are able to aggregate assets or flow to a higher level than a firm itself, as these activities are not within the firm's own primary capabilities.

## Relational View

This view argues that there are certain shortcomings in the two former perspectives. Thus, this view draws from both perspectives and adds the dimension of synergies in simultaneous learning through partnerships. The relational perspective thus focuses on creating value through partnerships. This value is created by sharing knowledge, capabilities, ideas etc. It is suggested that the reason for outsourcing primarily is based on the desire to acquire new knowledge through inter-firm learning. This implies that a firm will only outsource when the relationship offers the opportunity of learning through exchange and sharing of resources (Mehta et al., 2006). This approach to the make-or-buy decision may be particularly relevant in the case of BPO where firms may be mutually interdependent and sharing of knowledge is essential. This perspective assumes that opportunistic behavior, which transaction cost theory is based on, does not exist. If opportunistic behavior were present, the advantages of exchanging and sharing resources would contain substantial risks. Outsourcing decisions may thus be driven by any one or a combination of these three perspectives focusing on costs, core competences and/or relational learning respectively. These three perspectives deal with the make-or-buy decision in general. In the following paragraph a more BPO-specific decision model for the make-or-buy decision will be presented.

## A Make-or-Buy Decision Model for Business Process Outsourcing

Dong-Hoon Yang et al. (2007) have created a reasonable and simple model to assist the decision-making process of BPO. This model identifies the important factors that affect the BPO decision and that therefore should be considered in the make-or-buy decision. The model is illustrated in Table 2.2.

*Table 2.2: Factors Affecting the BPO Make-or-Buy Decision*

| Goal | Evaluating Weights of Factors Affecting BPO Decision | | |
|------|-----------------|------------------|-----------|
| Criteria | *Expectations* | *Risks* | *Environment* |
| Sub-criteria | Cost savings | Information security | Supplier's service quality |
| | Focus on core competences | Loss of control | |
| | Flexibility | Labor union | |
| | | Morale problem | |

Source: Own compilation inspired by Dong-HoonYang et al. (2007, p. 3771)

Historically, decisions about BPO were often made primarily based on costs. In recent years, however, there has been increased recognition of the need to take a wide range of other factors into account as well (Dong-Hoon Yang et al., 2007). Dong-Hoon Yang et al. (2007) therefore present three criteria for BPO evaluation: 1) Expectations, 2) Risks, and 3) Environment, each with a number of sub-criteria.

*Expectation Criteria.* Under this criterion, the earlier presented criteria *transaction cost and focus on core-competences* are presented as sub-criteria. The last sub-criterion is *flexibility,* which refers to firms' expectations about how service suppliers can adapt to needs of their clients' and markets and provide suitable services to satisfy client expectations. Outsourcing non-core activities also increases flexibility through the better use of internal resources. It enables quick responsiveness to customer needs, and decreases financial risks by reducing capital investments. Hence cost savings, focus on core competences and flexibility in management are the primary reasons for outsourcing a business process.

*Risk Criteria.* Alongside the expected benefits, the firm must also consider the shortcomings/risks of outsourcing, which could lead to an undesirable outcome. The two biggest risks in BPO are *information-security* concerns and *loss of management control.* These two factors could be coupled with hidden costs which also are represented in transaction cost theory regarding opportunism. For a supplier to be able to perform the contracted activities efficiently, information must be shared between the two firms, forcing the client to share sensitive information. Therefore, information security is a serious issue, particularly in the case of BPO, because BPO suppliers are not just agencies for simple processes, but entities that manage whole outsourcing processes. If the objectives of a BPO firm and its suppliers are not aligned, loss of management control over the supplier can occur. Therefore, it is critical to the success of the partnership for both parties to clarify their goals and expectations.

*Environment Perspective.* The third and last criterion is the external environment, which focuses on supplier service quality. Firms considering BPO must rigorously evaluate their capabilities in relation to their suppliers. After this analysis, the firm eliminates any potential suppliers that are unsuitable for the activities it intends to outsource. If the firm finds a suitable partner, it should form a partnership while leveraging its own capabilities. Most managers consider BPO when they believe that there is a significant difference in the quality of service provided by the suppliers compared to internal resources. Good quality of services is one of the most important success factors of BPO.

The three criteria, divided into eight sub-criteria which have been presented above, provide a good framework for firms considering BPO. By including additional factors that affect BPO adoption other than just cost savings, the pitfalls of the classic outsourcing decision presented in transaction-cost theory can be avoided. This will furthermore ensure that the decision has been considered in a more long-term planning perspective. The framework thus provides managers with guidelines on the factors that can affect their BPO make-or-buy decision.

**The Location Decision**

Following the make-or-buy decision, the location decision arises. This is where the location to perform the given activity is chosen based on the attractiveness of the location. This paragraph will present which factors affect a location's attractiveness and, further, which moderating factors influence the location decision. As shown in Figure 2.2, the location decision can both be relevant when the firm decides to perform the activity in-house or when it decides to outsource the activity, as many of the same factors affect the location decision disregarding the mode of ownership.

## Dunning's Eclectic Paradigm

When considering international production, the eclectic paradigm, also known as the OLI framework, is widely accepted. It focuses on how firms decide whether to engage in foreign activities, where to engage these and how.

The OLI framework contains three criteria that must be present in order to engage in foreign activities: (O)wnership advantages, (L)ocation advantages and (I)nternalization advantages (Lüthje, 2005). Ownership

43

advantages are capabilities that are unique to the firm. These determine whether the firm should engage in international activities at all. Location advantages are the capabilities of a given country/area equally accessible to all firms. These include macro-economic factors which are divided into infrastructure, country risk and government policy (Graf and Mudambi, 2005). These variables can be seen as a consequence of the difference in the countries' factor proportion (Lüthje, 2005). Hence, location advantages decide where the firm should place its activity, thus focusing on the location decision. Internalization advantages determine the mode of ownership, i.e. whether the firm should employ off-shoring or off-shore outsourcing. Internalization advantages can be described as the advantages acquired by performing the activity within the hierarchy when locating the activity in a foreign location, instead of acquiring the activity through the market (Dicken, 2007).

The OLI framework contributes in particular to the location decision seen in an outsourcing context, by suggesting which factors to evaluate (infrastructure, country risk and government policy) when considering the location of the firm's activities. As this classic paradigm originally focuses on foreign direct investments, i.e. not outsourcing directly, and merely on production activities than business processes, further theoretical insights into the location decision of BPO will be necessary.

## Location Decision Model for Business Process Outsourcing

In order to apply Dunning's location decision dimensions to the context of BPO, Graf and Mudambi (2005) add a human capital dimension and moderating factors to Dunning's OLI framework. Thus, this model specifically focuses on where to outsource to, i.e. the location decision based on location attractiveness. As mentioned earlier, Dunning identified three determinants of location: 1) Infrastructure, 2) Country risk, and 3) Government policy. His framework does however not include human capital dimensions. In the context of business processes, human capital is a very important factor due to the role of the "human touch" in service activities. Besides adding a human capital dimension, Graf and Mudambi (2005) include moderating effects of firm-specific factors and situation-specific factors. This decision model is illustrated in Figure 2.4. Following this, it is unclear whether and under what conditions firms make the location choice prior to making their partner choice. In some cases the partner might influence or even make the final choice, which will undermine the importance of the location decision factors. Hence, the analysis of the location decision will be based on making the location choice prior to the partner choice.

*Figure 2.4: Factors Affecting Location Attractiveness*

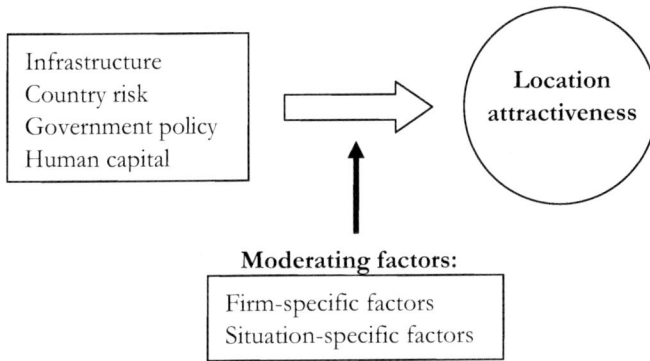

Source: Own compilation, inspired by Graf and Mudambi (2005, p.258)

*Infrastructure.* Availability and quality of IT-infrastructure and competitive costs of IT are significant requirements for an attractive BPO location. Thus, the role of the physical infrastructure network is a less significant factor in a BPO context, as no physical transportation is needed. However, geographic distance can be a factor to consider regarding time differences and coordination.

*Country Risk.* Country risk involves both economic and political risk. Measures of economic risk include openness of the economic system, inflation rates, and exchange rate fluctuations, while political risks include political instability, conflicts between nations and the likelihood of changes in regulation and laws affecting business and trade. The general assumption to consider is the more change, the more risk.

*Government Policy.* Governments have the ability to affect foreign involvement in service industries by imposing obstacles and discriminatory barriers or by providing incentives through tax and fiscal instruments and subsidies.

*Human Capital.* BPO involves a balance of information technologies and the human touch. This is the argument for adding the human capital dimension in the context of BPO. Human capital involves five factors: availability, experience, quality, compensation level and cultural distance. *Availability* deals with the size of the labor pool, which needs to be

45

sufficiently large to meet the necessary operating hours. Secondly, the labor pool's BPO *experience* is of interest. Thus, a well-trained and experienced work-force is a highly valuable resource. Thirdly, the human resources need to be of appropriate *quality* in order to support customer needs. Quality of human labor involves technical expertise and interpersonal aspects such as language competence, understandability or strength of the accent. Fourth, in a competitive marketplace, the *compensation level* of employees also affects the BPO location choice, as the difference in labor costs between the home market and the BPO location can be highly significant. Finally, *cultural distance* plays a role in shaping employee attitudes toward technology, customers and interpersonal contact, and culture affects employees' role perception.

Firm-specific and situation-specific factors moderate the direct effects of these four categories of determinants. It is thus specific for the given firm and situation which of the location determinants is most important.

*Moderating Factors*. Besides the direct effects of the four dimensions mentioned above, moderating factors have the potential to affect the impact of infrastructure, country risk, government policy and human capital on the perception of location attractiveness, and thereby on the location decision. Moderating factors can be divided into firm-specific and situation-specific factors.

*Firm-specific factors* deal with the fact that different firms may have different objectives for BPO e.g. cost-reduction, business process improvement and capability enhancement. These three objectives are coherent with the three theoretical perspectives: transaction cost theory, competence-base view and the relational view. Given these differences in objectives, it could be rationalized that a firm which seeks capability enhancement will prioritize human capital higher. Besides the firm's objectives, international experience and outsourcing experience can also influence location choices for BPO.

*Situation-specific factors* can be divided into two factors, the nature of the business process and customer expectations. The nature of the business process can be described by: strategic importance, process standardization/complexity, asset specificity and visibility to customers. These can for example be influenced by putting more weight on country risk for more strategically important processes and less weight on human capital for highly standardized processes. Customer expectations can likewise be a moderating factor through interpersonal interaction and convenience. For example for business processes such as technical service support and customer care (front-office processing), the customer expects considerable interpersonal interaction and convenience in getting this.

As described, this model presents four dimensions that affect location attractiveness and how these can be influenced by moderating factors. Hätönen (2009) has presented a similar model for location choice, which contains the same elements as Graf and Mudambi's (2005) conceptual model for location decision. However, Hätönen (2009) ascribes greater importance to the moderating factors. According to Hätönen (2009), the primary factors behind the decision are not location-specific, such as infrastructure, country risk, government policy and human capital, but rather situational and internal, in the sense of what is being outsourced and why, and what kind of experience the firm processes. Thus, the nature of the outsourcing activity and the outsourcing objective has the primary influence on the location decision. The moderating factors can, besides influencing the location decision, also influence the choice of partner. For example, if the objective is cost savings, the choice of location precedes the choice of partner. Vice versa, if the objective is either capability enhancement or process improvement, the choice of partner will precede the choice of location.

## Research Questions

The theoretical perspectives on outsourcing are the point of reference for the research questions to be presented in this paragraph. Therefore, the research questions can be traced directly to the reviewed theories. Research question 1 deals with the make-or-buy decision. Research question 2 captures the moderating factors affecting the location factors. Finally, location factors are investigated in detail in research questions 3 and 4.

**Research Question 1:** *What is the most common objective for initiating outsourcing/off-shoring of business processes to India?*

- Which objective (cost reduction, focus on core competences, learning) is predominant for foreign firms in moving business processes to India?
- Are there any other objectives for foreign firms in moving business processes to India?

**Research Question 2:** *What is the nature of business processes performed by suppliers in India?*

- Which type of business processes are undertaken in India (front-, middle- and back-office)?
- How complex are the business processes undertaken by suppliers in India?
- How experienced in outsourcing activities are firms that move activities to India?

**Research Question 3:** *What is the role of human capital factors in the location decision for firms outsourcing/off-shoring business processes to India?*

- How important are human capital factors (availability, experience, quality, compensation level and cultural distance) for foreign firms that move business processes to India?
- Which of these provide the main challenges for suppliers in India?

**Research Question 4:** *Which location factors cause the most significant challenges for the BPO industry?*

- Are there any IT-infrastructural challenges in India affecting BPO?
- Are there any political and economic risks in India affecting BPO?
- Are there any Governmental challenges in India affecting BPO?

## Methodology

This chapter consists of two main parts. The first part is mainly theoretical, and has been based primarily on a literature review. These articles have been found through the search engine, EBSCO, which searches across several scientific journals and magazines. "BPO India" has been used as search term, and the results were limited to only include reviewed full texts with references available published in the period from 2000 to 2009. This search resulted in 12836 hits, which have been prioritized after relevance to the search words and the date of publishing. Through screening of headings and/or abstracts a satisfying number of 25 relevant scientific articles were selected. This has provided a basic understanding of BPO and several aspects around the topic. Furthermore, it has served as a solid knowledgebase and framework in order to gather the primary empirical data necessary for the second part of this chapter.

In gathering empirical data a case study approach has been applied. The goal is not to generalize, but to search for dominant tendencies concerning BPO in India. When visiting the firms, semi-structured face-to-face interviews and the firms' own introductions have been the primary sources of data. As the data gathered primarily is of qualitative nature, the data will of course only be treated as such. It is in other words not the intention to transform the qualitative data into measurable quantitative data. This approach is chosen as it is not the intention to generalize, but merely to search for dominant tendencies concerning BPO in India. Furthermore, the individual firms will not be mentioned by name or as fictive case references, as the case study is focused on searching for dominant tendencies based on a limited generalization from the six interviews. For this reason, there will not be a reference for the source of each presented fact. All facts in the next paragraph are derived from the six interviews. Hence these are the only sources of information.

## Empirical Studies

Our empirical studies are based on six visits at five firms and one NGO in India. During these visits, qualitative semi-structured interviews, with the different actors representing the individual firms, were conducted. Through these interviews, it is attempted to find tendencies concerning BPO in India and thereby answer the following four research questions.

> **Research Question 1:** *What is the most common objective/motive for initiating outsourcing/off-shoring of business processes to India?*

This paragraph will attempt to answer the overall question, why do firms outsource or off-shore business processes to India? Through the literature review, three predominant objectives for outsourcing and/or off-shoring have been found. These predominant objectives are cost reduction, focus on core-competences, and learning. Besides these three objectives, the empirical findings show additional objectives, which of course also will be discussed. Finally, it will be discussed whether there are any differences in these objectives between firms that outsource and firms that off-shore business processes to India.

> *Which objective (cost reduction, focus on core competences, learning) is predominant for foreign firms in moving business processes to India?*

The empirical studies show that cost reduction is the most significant objective when moving business processes to India. The price of labor is in some industries only 1/10 compared to Western standards, which of course is a strong motivator. However, productivity is not quite as high as in the Western world. Still, the empirical studies found that costs can be reduced by around 60 percent compared to US suppliers undertaking similar activities. In other words, India has a great comparative advantage in terms of the price of labor. However, India is a large economy in rapid growth, expecting annual growth rates of around 8 percent until the year 2020. This rapid growth rate will influence the cost of labor, which will converge towards Western levels and over time reduce India's comparative labor cost advantage through inevitably higher inflation rates. Due to this, in the long run, cost reduction by itself will not be a sufficient foundation for moving business processes to India anymore, simply because other countries can become more attractive in relation to labor costs. Therefore, for off-shoring or outsourcing to be sustainable over time, the strategy has to be value-adding to the firm. Value can be added in different ways, but the focus in this section will be on core competences and learning.

Outsourcing or off-shoring of peripheral activities can release resources, which may be better used by focusing on core-competences in the home country. Typically, this could for example be R&D or design. Focusing on what the firm does best can therefore be value-adding and help the firm achieve a competitive edge. This kind of thinking was also dominant among the firms visited during the empirical data gathering in India. Besides costs, most of the visited firms mentioned focus on core-competences as a very important motive for moving business processes to India.

The third objective is learning. Learning in this context relates to gathering knowledge about the Indian market, culture etc. with the motive of entering the Indian market. This is supported by the empirical studies, which showed that most firms with the intention of penetrating the Indian market focused on the learning aspect. At the same time, a strong tendency towards off-shoring among these firms was found. According to these firms, off-shoring provides a much stronger basis for doing business in India than outsourcing, because presence of the firm is the most effective way to learn about the market. Learning, however, is not a predominant factor for firms, which do not consider entering the Indian sales market, but which just perform certain activities in India. The reason for this is the Indian culture and mindset, which does not encourage innovative thinking. This point will be further discussed in research question 3.

Summing up the discussion of these three predominant objectives for moving business processes to India, it can be concluded that they are indeed all three important objectives. However, cost reduction seems to be the most common objective, while focusing on core-competences is secondary. Learning mainly seems to be important for firms off-shoring to India with the intention of entering the market. However, in the long run it is not sustainable to focus on cost advantage alone when moving activities to India.

*Are there any other objectives for foreign firms in moving business processes to India?*

The objectives for moving business processes to India discussed above were inspired by the literature review. However, the empirical studies revealed additional objectives, which will be presented and discussed in this section.

When Western firms started moving business processes to India in the early 1990's, one of the reasons was the time difference. The time difference was mainly a reason for US firms, as Indian office hours started when American office hours ended. This meant that US firms could have activities carried out in India overnight, which then could be ready the next morning. The time difference has never been a motive for European firms, because it does not provide substantial advantages as it does between Indian and American firms. Today, the time difference is not that important as many jobs are carried out in real time regardless of the time difference. Thereby, the time difference is more of a challenge than an advantage.

An important objective found through the empirical studies is the sales opportunities in the Indian market. Even though India has 350 million people living below the international poverty limit, there still is a very large consumer market. For example, India has a growing middle class consisting of 300 million people and will be the world's 5th largest consumer market by 2025. By moving business processes to India, the distance to market issue can be minimized. Additionally, it provides firms with the opportunity to learn and explore the Indian market with the intension of sales. This point was made by the majority of the visited firms during the empirical study in India and must therefore be considered an extremely important objective, almost as important as the earlier discussed cost reduction possibilities. However, it is important to understand the differences in Indian customers needs compared to Western countries. In India, basic physical and security needs are of high importance as they are not completely fulfilled for a large percentage of the population. Therefore, Indian firms and consumers will often focus primarily on short-term cash flow rather than long-term sustainability. A mistake which Western firms must avoid in this matter, is the mistake of "overdesigning" their products and services. This means that the products and services should not be loaded with features and services that, even though they are normal in the Western countries, will be viewed as unnecessary by Indian firms and consumers who will find them too expensive. This must be avoided to be able to compete with very cost-focused local Indian firms.

Another objective found in the empirical studies is the availability of a very large and well-skilled workforce. Especially a strong pool of engineers, but also scientists and law graduates are available. This compared with the fact that these kinds of employees can be hired for a fraction of the costs in the Western world provides India with a strong comparative advantage. Lack of employees like engineers, scientists and law graduates in some parts of the Western world strengthen India's comparative advantage in the context of the workforce. This well-skilled workforce is also one of the parameters that differentiate India from for example China. In China, the workforce might also be large, available and cheap, but educational levels are not nearly as high as in India. A final factor in the context of the workforce and Indians in general are their good English skills dating back from the time when India was a British colony. This makes communication a lot less problematic than in other Asian countries, like for example China.

As a final comment to this paragraph about moving business processes to India, the differences in objectives, whether a firm outsources or off-shores activities will be discussed. During the literature review and empirical studies, five objectives for moving business processes to India were discovered. These five objectives are costs, focus on core-competences, learning, market attractiveness, and large skilled workforce. The question is now whether a firm should outsource or off-shore. The empirical studies show that there is a strong tendency towards off-shoring, which mainly is due to market learning opportunities, market attractiveness and a large skilled workforce. The presence of these three factors is what separates India from other Asian countries. Off-shoring also allows firms to move increasingly complex business processes, more so than traditional outsourcing because it provides a higher degree of control of the activities carried out. In the context of outsourcing, the overall dominant objective is cost reduction, by having foreign suppliers undertake relatively simple and standardized processes. If cost reduction is the only objective for moving business processes, other countries than India might in time be more attractive, which makes this a short-term solution.

The question of whether a firm should outsource or off-shore their activities to India, also greatly depends on the type of activities; a matter which will be discussed further in research question two.

**Research Question 2:** *What is the nature of business processes performed by suppliers in India?*

As the focus of this chapter is on business process outsourcing, the nature of the business processes performed in India was also investigated through the empirical study. This is an interesting focus area because this depends on the capabilities of the BPO industry in India and the country's overall competitiveness. According to Figure 2.1, business processes can be classified by both the type of activity and the complexity of the activity. These two classifications and their implications will be discussed in the following two sub-questions.

*Which type of business processes is undertaken by suppliers in India (front-, middle- and back-office)?*

In the empirical study, it was discovered which kind of actual activities the notion of front-, middle- and back-office activities mainly consist of in India.

*Front-Office Activities.* Front-office activities are activities with direct customer interaction. The starting point of outsourcing business processes to India was call centers. This was a simple form of direct selling to customers all over the world. In line with the rising attractiveness of the Indian consumer market, direct selling has taken a more focused form. Foreign firms that pursue sales opportunities in India now tend to establish local sales offices to achieve close contact with the customer. For the same reason, foreign firms are starting to establish more after sales activities locally as well. The development within front-office activities performed in India is moving towards a more local and close contact approach rather than the transaction based approach which is seen in the call centers.

*Middle-Office Activities.* Middle-office activities have lower direct customer interaction. The empirical study did not put much effort into middle-office activities, as the extremes of front-office and back-office activities arguably provide more valuable insights. Figure 2.1 illustrates some examples of middle-office activities, such as telecom services, insurance and banking.

*Back-Office Activities.* In back-office activities, there is usually no direct contact with the customer. The most essential back-office activity for many firms is R&D. This is however not so predominant in the BPO industry in India, due to the less innovative Indian mindset. Therefore, R&D activities in India are mostly performed by foreign firms establishing an in-house off-shore location in India and only seldom through outsourcing activities to Indian suppliers. The reason for this tendency is that innovation and learning often has to arise at the parent firm or at least in cooperation with the parent firm. The more typical back-office activities performed in India are activities within finance, IT solutions and legal services. These activities can and often do function as back-office for the parent firms' total global activities. In this way, the parent firm can benefit from economies of scale on a global level. These back-office activities are in India often described as knowledge processes. These processes need a higher educated workforce as the processes are more knowledge based.

The present development in India is moving towards more focus upstream in the value chain on back-office activities. This is in accordance with the high focus on education and the trend toward providing more knowledge-based processes. Even though back-office activities require more knowledge, the complexity still varies.

*How complex are the business processes undertaken by suppliers in India?*

The empirical study made it clear that activities that are outsourced to India are mainly standard routinized processes. In Figure 2.1 this kind of low complexity activities were defined as discrete processes. Even though more back-office activities are being outsourced to India, the complexity of these activities are still relatively low. The reason for this is that these knowledge processes are based more on knowledge than on creativity and innovative thinking. Knowledge processes need more educational knowledge in the business area, but applying this to the same non-innovative mindset, these processes will still be standardized, just on a higher level. For this reason innovative thinking has to take place at the parent firm. Therefore, there seems to be coherence between the complexity of the process and the choice between outsourcing and off-shoring. As innovative thinking mainly has to take place at the parent firm, off-shoring is more predominant for processes of a high complexity. The reason for this is that the collaboration between parent firm and supplier is much closer in off-shoring than in outsourcing, which encourages learning between the partners. In off-shoring on the other hand, innovative thinking mainly arises in the parent

54

firm and if any innovative activities are performed by the Indian supplier, it is closely monitored by the parent firm. The main focus for innovation in India is on providing input to market-specific adaptations. This local presence is an important opportunity for the parent firm when pursuing increasing market shares in a rapidly growing consumer market.

*How experienced in outsourcing activities are firms that move activities to India?*

To explore why outsourcing/off-shoring activities to India are of interest, it would be relevant to characterize the type of firms that successfully have accomplished this. The primary distinctive characteristic is the size of the firm. Often foreign firms present in India are relatively large. The reason for this is that these firms find the movement of activities to India a considerably large investment in a long-term strategy. That could also be a reason why off-shoring is more predominant than outsourcing.

Moreover these firms are not first-time outsourcers, but are often present in other countries as well. An example of this are firms that combine high- volume/low-margin products in China with low-volume/high-margin products in India. This suggests that even though China is often seen as a competitor to India in attracting foreign firms, these two countries can be used in a complementing combination.

**Research Question 3:** *What is the role of human capital factors in the location decision for firms outsourcing/off-shoring business processes to India?*

Having mentioned some of the main drivers for moving business processes to India, it is time to focus more specifically on the human capital factors influencing the outsourcing and off-shoring decision. The importance of human capital as a driver of BPO was discovered in research question 1, as the size and skill level of the Indian workforce was found to be a motive to move business processes to India. Therefore a more detailed analysis of these human capital factors will follow.

*How important are human capital factors (availability, experience, quality, compensation level and cultural distance) for foreign firms that move business processes to India?*

As mentioned earlier, it is a driver for most foreign firms that India has a large labor force. There are more than 2 million university graduates each year; hence, there are many possibilities for foreign firms to employ skilled employees. Most of these graduates are IT-specialists, engineers and scientists. Hence, the availability and quality of the workforce are important human capital factors in India, in which it seems that India is already excelling. Moreover, there is great focus on continuous training, especially accent training for front-office activities. Even though most Indians have great English skills, their accent is often affected by their local language.

With respect to general skills, it is very difficult to make a direct comparison to Western countries in relation to the quality of the graduates and furthermore the experience of the workforce. Experience varies, but still the possibilities and availability of very skilled and educated employees is huge. Regarding the experience of the workforce, it is difficult to make one single conclusion. There are many very experienced workers in India, but the main part of these workers have gathered knowledge and worked outside of India for a short period of time. In this way, they understand the Western way of doing business. On the other hand, work experience in India may seem low when looking at the whole country in general. This could be a result of the poverty level. Furthermore, the age composition of the Indian population at this moment is very young, as one third of the population is younger than 15 years.

Besides size, skills and experience of the workforce, foreign firms which are either present in India now or firms which plan to off-shore or outsource activities to India have to be very aware of cultural differences. Culture is perhaps the most important human capital factor, as it affects whether the foreign firm will be able to capture the advantages of the size and skills of the workforce. Hence, culture has a great impact on the other human capital factors.

*Which of these factors provide the main challenges for suppliers in India?*

While the workforce is large and the skills of the workforce are improving, cultural differences provide the main challenges for foreign firms outsourcing or off-shoring to India. Looking at cultural differences, Indians and Indian firms differ in many ways from most Western firms. Hence, culture should be seen as the main challenge when doing business in India. For instance it is rare to experience an Indian answering "no" if you put forward a proposal or an idea. This means that they always say yes, even though they know that what they are being asked to do is impossible. Of course, this creates many situations that a foreign firm has to be aware of when for instance negotiating or doing business in general. Furthermore, when negotiating, it is important to establish a relationship with the Indian counterpart, instead of moving directly to the point as Western firms often tend to do, as relationships are of great importance in India. Deadlines are another issue that creates problems, which is closely related to the "saying-no dilemma". This means that they will not tell you if they are unable to meet a deadline, they will just accept at first and then later ask for postponement. This makes it necessary for one to confirm an agreement several times to be sure it will be met. Another important cultural issue is that Indians do not tend to "think outside the box", because they are often risk averse. For this reason, Indian firms do not pursue innovative thinking and do not make innovation part of their goals or strategy. This affects how foreign firms should operate in India. This means that instead of being innovative and creative, they just do things in the exact same way every single time. In this way, Indian workers are usually only performing tasks that are standardized and in relation to BPO the complexity of the various tasks are limited, as mentioned in research question 2. Hence, it would not be obvious to place an R&D department in India. The empirical study did show examples of R&D activities placed in India and other forms of innovative thinking. However, in all these cases it was a case of off-shoring rather than outsourcing. This means that the foreign firm has to impose innovation and development on the Indian partner, as it requires a change of mindset, which often is not possible in a more transactional outsourcing approach. This indicates that it is possible to help Indian firms to be more innovative through a close collaboration with the foreign firm. This again would most often require that the foreign firm chooses the off-shoring approach, instead of the outsourcing approach.

Taking the above mentioned examples of cultural differences into consideration, the best way to do business with Indians is to build and create a relationship. This takes time, but in the end you will get a better understanding of the overall differences regarding the cultural aspects affecting the Indian way of doing business.

**Research Question 4:** *Which location factors cause the most significant challenges for the BPO industry?*

India is a country of contrasts and although there are many advantages in the vast BPO industry, there are certainly also numerous challenges. Before considering going to India, one must bear in mind not only the cultural differences, but also that India is split into three centuries of development: it is a mixture of the 19th, 20th and 21th century. The apparent problems this brings forward are the key to the most significant problems for the BPO industry in the 21st century.

*Are there any IT-infrastructural challenges in India affecting BPO?*

Reliable IT-infrastructure is a necessity for BPO that most foreign firms expect present. In an Indian perspective, challenges in this area can both be present or not, this is therefore not a question easily answered. This stems from which angle one chooses to look at this particular issue. For example broadband in India may not be the quality and speed as one could and would expect from a Western point of view. Likewise, electricity is of somewhat unreliable nature which makes it necessary to have one's own power generators within the firm. However problematic this may appear, there is some sort of agreement on this topic; that this is not a problem which cannot be solved in the near future. The motive for this conclusion is that the Government is making large investments in the IT-infrastructure, which already has caused great improvements in this area. On the other hand physical infrastructure is a huge problem in India, not only in the vast rural areas, which makes it immensely difficult to simply move commodities from one location to another. This is not only due to the poor infrastructure, but also due to the fact that India consists of different states with different laws and different plans on how to develop infrastructure. One of the major prevailing challenges of infrastructure are urban rather than rural, since the urban areas are growing at a rate that makes urban planning almost redundant. Cities grow every day and they can simply not accommodate the increasing number of people. This puts a growing strain on the city's infrastructure and rigid local governments make planning a long process. This means that by the time all parties agree and action can be taken, new problems have arisen and the plan is no longer sufficient to solve the problems. Poor physical infrastructure puts a strain on workers and managers, because getting to and from work is a slow affair. Again, this has a direct effect on employees' productivity. This makes the physical infrastructure a present challenge, even in a BPO context where the issue of IT-infrastructure normally is more predominant. Whether or not the Indian government is able to vastly improve and cope with these challenges is the big question. Otherwise, both Indian and foreign firms will not be able to fully harvest any of the other benefits of the country.

The time of the protectionist Indian economy of the 1980's is over and India is now considered an open economy with a low level of trade barriers. This openness arose throughout the 1990's, starting with a liberalization of the Indian economy in order to attract foreign direct investments in the IT industry, known as the IT boom. It is on the continuation of this IT boom that the present BPO industry relies. It has provided an open economy and a focus on promoting outsourcing from foreign firms. For example, the Indian Government establishes knowledge centers and centers of excellence to promote the development of the BPO industry. This provides great locational advantages contributing to the country's competitiveness. Furthermore, India is a relatively stable democracy. This however brings along a very high level of bureaucracy, which slows down the Government's decision-making. The Indian democracy is a slow moving organ with numerous departments and it can be difficult for foreign firms to navigate through the Indian bureaucracy jungle. Also, legislation is different from state to state, the taxation levels on goods are different, and it is necessary to acquire separate state licenses to trade. This problem is of course more important for firms selling or manufacturing commodities in India.

The Indian economy has been characterized mainly by a very high annual growth rate (close to 10 percent). This of course causes many opportunities, but also affects the inflation rate and eventually the cost advantage. The inflation rate in India is higher than in the Western countries (approximately 5-6 percent) which in the long run will cause a convergence toward Western economies. This will over time diminish the level of the present cost advantage in India. Foreign firms considering moving activities to India should take this into consideration, as moving activities to India purely motivated by cost advantage will be shortsighted.

*Are there any governmental challenges in India affecting BPO?*

Governmental factors deal with subsidies and trading taxes. It has already been mentioned that taxes vary from state to state, which can cause a lack of transparency for foreign firms. On the other hand, the Indian Government provides tax holidays, where specific firms are exempted for paying tax for periods of several years. These tax holidays are typically industry specific, and will therefore not be discussed in further detail here.

Another issue addressed in the empirical study was corruption. Diverse views on whether corruption should be regarded as a problem in doing business in India were discovered. The issue was both seen as a predominant problem and as non-existing. Therefore, no clear conclusion can be drawn on this subject. However, foreign firms considering moving activities to India should be aware that this issue may be a challenge to face.

## Empirical Overview

The analysis of human capital (research question 3) and location factors (research question 4) in India clearly shows that these are fundamentals to why a firm would choose to move activities to India (research question 1) and to which activities that should be moved to India (research question 2). The reason for this is that these (human capital and location factors) are the basis for both the advantages and the challenges of the country, determining the country's overall competitiveness, thereby creating opportunities to benefit from and obstacles to overcome.

# Conclusion

This conclusion will pinpoint the main findings of the study. Afterwards, these findings will be summarized in the context of practical implications. The main findings of this study are achieved through four main research questions derived from the literature study on business process outsourcing.

The first research question indicated that cost reduction is the most significant objective for foreign firms to move activities to India. Despite cost reductions, focus on core competences is becoming a more prevailing objective. This is a consequence of globalization, which increases competition and requires a focus on specialization in the firms' core competences. Learning, however, is not a dominant objective to move activities to India, because of the less innovative Indian mindset. Learning is mainly relevant for firms that view India as a sales market, where learning is essential regarding understanding Indian market needs. Thereby also implying that sales opportunities alone are an important motive to move activities to India. Another motive discovered in the study was the large and skilled workforce, which distinguishes India from other developing countries. In this way, the availability and quality of the workforce can be viewed as an objective to move activities to India, even though the scientific literature only regards this as a location factor influencing the location decision, and not the make-or-buy decision.

Differences in firms' objectives were discovered between outsourcing and off-shoring strategies. Outsourcing strategies mainly focused on achieving cost reductions, as this can be seen as a short-term advantage. Beside cost reductions, off-shoring strategies also focused on sales opportunities and learning in this context, as learning requires closer control over foreign activities. The reason for this is that close control is necessary to capture full advantage of learning, market attractiveness and the large skilled workforce.

Research question 2 discussed the difference between the types of activities and the complexity of these. The BPO industry in India started mainly by providing front-office activities, but has developed to also include back-office activities where the processes are still standardized just on a higher knowledge level. These processes are characterized as knowledge processes and mainly consist of processes within finance, IT and legal services. Again, differences between outsourcing and off-shoring strategies were discovered. The tendency was primarily that more complex processes were off-shored, rather than outsourced.

Research question 3 regarded the importance of different human capital factors. When moving business processes to India, the most important human capital factors influencing the location decision were labor availability and quality of the workforce. A more challenging human capital factor discovered was cultural distance. The cultural challenges consist mainly of issues regarding unwillingness to say "no", failing to fulfill deadlines, the importance of establishing and maintaining relationships and the inability to "think outside the box".

Research question 4 covered the last factors influencing the location decision. Problems regarding IT-infrastructure include instability and power interruptions. Overall, improvements of the IT-infrastructure are developing in a positive direction at a reasonable pace. Therefore, these are minor problems compared to the poor physical infrastructure, which affects workers' productivity negatively.

Politically, the main problem is the widespread democracy. Obviously, a stable democracy is an advantage in maintaining political stability, however in India, democracy also brings along very bureaucratic authorities. Therefore, changes and improvements are a slow process, which can cause establishment of a new division in India to result in a significant start-up time. Economically, the high inflation rate caused by the economic growth should be considered. This will in time diminish cost advantages due to convergence towards Western cost levels, which will make an outsourcing or off-shoring strategy purely based on cost advantages a short-term strategy.

**Implications**

The findings of this study have several implications for firms considering moving business processes to India, based on the discovered opportunities to benefit from and the challenges to overcome. The most important are summarized in Table 2.3.

*Table 2.3: Opportunities and Challenges*

| Opportunities | Challenges |
|---|---|
| • Lower costs (short-term) | • Cultural distance |
| • Market attractiveness | • Low innovative capabilities |
| • Size and skills of workforce | • Bureaucracy |

Source: Own compilation

These opportunities and challenges determine, in combination with the specific firm and situation, which strategy approach to follow when moving business processes to India.

*An outsourcing strategy* can be beneficial when the objective is cost reduction with a short-term focus and the outsourced processes are of relatively low complexity. Furthermore, the challenges caused by the bureaucratic nature of Indian authorities are partly avoided through an outsourcing strategy, because the firm cooperates with an already established firm.

*An off-shoring strategy* can be beneficial when the objective is not only cost reduction. An off-shoring strategy can also capture long-term advantages within a combination of sales opportunities and learning. Furthermore, an off-shoring strategy may fully benefit from the advantages of the large and skilled workforce as these become embedded in the organization. Additionally, an off-shoring strategy is also useful in moving complex and knowledge-based processes, as the parent firm can retain control and impose innovation and development upon the off-shore division. Moreover, an off-shoring strategy approach will presumably increase the firms' abilities to understand and cope with the cultural differences.

# CHAPTER 3

# Business Clusters and Localization in Southern India

Thomas Dittmann, Anders Ilsøe, René H. Larsen, Elsi Thoumy and Kinga Tonak

## Abstract

*The purpose of this chapter is to identify and discuss benefits that companies are able to gain by participating in cluster activities and from their location, when doing business in Southern India. This contribution is especially intended for Danish companies that are considering locating to this area. This study provides empirical insights, gathered from interviews with four companies located in Bangalore and Chennai. It was found that Danish companies need to consider issues along a wide spectrum, like for instance access to skilled labor, infrastructure, legislation, competitors and suppliers location, and existing triple helix cooperation, in order to be successful.*

## Introduction

Through the years, there has been a development in the way humans think. From the early days when companies did most of the production on their own, not sharing much with their suppliers and business associates, up until today, where companies for instance rely on their suppliers and business associates to innovate and develop new products. Companies even want to move part of their production to geographical places where the concentration of companies in the same industry is high. This way of thinking is called clustering and localization, and has been an important study for years - and remains so today.

Clustering has been discussed since the work of Marshall in 1930. Later on, researchers like Becattini (1990), Storper (1995), Porter (1998), Etzkowitz and Leydesdorff (2000), and Martin and Sunley (2003) have contributed further to the development of the cluster concept. In this chapter, the descriptions and analyses of cluster definition are based on Porter (2008):

> *"Clusters are geographic concentrations of inter-connected companies, specialized suppliers, service providers, firms in related industries, and associated institutions (for example, universities, standards agencies, and trade associations) in particular fields that compete, but also cooperate."*
> (Porter, 2008, p. 213)

Derived from this definition, the general idea behind clustering is that companies at the same time cooperate and compete in order to gain several advantages. These advantages may among other things be economic growth, job creation, innovation, and increased competitiveness. Moreover, Porter (2008) stresses the importance of other actors, such as knowledge institutions and trade associations, being present in clusters.

Since India is an attractive location for Danish companies, this chapter aims at merging the ideas of clustering and localization, in order to identify and portray cluster activity in Southern India, and to discuss how Danish companies located there can benefit from this. In accordance with this purpose the following research question is posed:

> *What can Danish companies learn from other companies' experience about location and cluster participation in Southern India?*

This chapter is structured in five main sections. The first section contains a presentation of the theoretical background with a focus on clusters and business localization. This section is followed by a description of the methodological techniques applied, in order to obtain the data necessary for answering the research question. The fourth section contains a discussion of the findings in the analysis. Finally, the chapter ends with a conclusion of the results obtained through this study.

## Literature Review

The purpose of this section is to provide a more extensive understanding of clustering and localization, with the intention of setting up a theoretical framework for answering the research question. The theoretical focus of this section is based on Porter's approach on clustering and Dunning's view on localization.

### What is a Cluster?

Based on the previously stated definition of a cluster, this section continues with Porter's (2008) contribution to the understanding of clusters. His work has been chosen, because it provides both a broad and comprehensible understanding of clusters. Moreover, his work contributes to localization theory, which is in consistence with Dunning's theory development.

According to Porter (2008), a basic definition of what constitutes a cluster is:

> *"...a geographically proximate group of interconnected companies and associated institutions in a particular field, linked by commonalities and complementarities. The geographic scope of a cluster can range from a single city or state to a country or even a network of neighboring countries."* (Porter, 2008, p. 215)

Regarding the scope of what constitutes a cluster, Porter (2008) explains the balance between grasping too widely and focusing too narrowly:

> *"... encompassing broad groupings, such as manufacturing, consumer goods, or high tech, have been too broadly conceived. Such aggregates exhibit, at best, weak connections among the industries included. ...Conversely, labeling a single industry as a cluster overlooks crucial cross-industry and institutional interconnections that strongly affect competitiveness."* (Porter, 2008, p. 218)

When drawing and defining the boundaries of a given cluster, it is important to remember that some of these participants may take part of several clusters (Porter, 2008). As an example, a metal manufacture may both supply parts to a wind turbine cluster and to an automobile cluster. Since clusters can vary in size, boundaries of the industries involved, as well as the number of participants, it is important to identify the entire group of companies involved in the cluster and by doing so, specify the boundaries of the cluster. The advantage for the individual company then is first of all the creation of an overview of the opportunities within the cluster, which can help the company better align its business strategy to operations in the given cluster. Second of all, it is important to know about all the actors within the cluster, with respect to creating close activity links, relationships ties and actor bonds. So to gain from the cluster advantages that will be described later, the company has to know wherefrom it can obtain these (Porter, 2008).

The geographic occurrence and location of clusters – in a demographic and macroeconomic perspective – is by Porter described as follows:

> *"They [clusters] are present in large and small economies, in rural and urban areas, and at several geographic levels (for example, nations, states, metropolitan regions, and cities). Clusters occur in both advanced and developing economies, although clusters in advanced economies tend to be far better developed."* (Porter, 2008, p. 220)

In other words, identifying the scope of an existing cluster can be quite a task in itself for companies wanting to relocate into the given area. Furthermore, Porter (2008) states that, through the years, location and competition has changed, due to the fact of competition becoming increasingly global. Companies therefore seek to link themselves to their buyers, suppliers and other institutions that provide and contribute to the increased productivity of the individual company. One of Porter's key points is exactly productivity, and the way companies gain from related companies, as well as from companies in other industries, when locating in a cluster.

Porter states that when participating in cluster activities, a company will benefit from different advantages, which are located within the geographical area of a cluster. This will be the subject for discussion in the following section.

## The Competitive Advantage of Clusters

The next step is to look at why it can be attractive for companies to locate themselves in a cluster. A major reason according to Porter is the pressure found in a climate of transparent competition, to continuously improve efficiency:

*"Coordination and internal pressures for improvement among parts of a cluster, made possible by co-location, can substantially improve its overall quality or efficiency."* (Porter, 2008, p. 233)

The following section will supply some main characteristics of a competitive cluster.

## Main Characteristics of a Competitive Cluster

After comprehending the basic concept of a cluster, and touching on the range of possible advantages from participating in one, it is then interesting to have a look at the characteristics, which Porter (2008) believes constitute the composition of an optimal cluster:

> *"...the breadth and depth of a cluster rather than the size of individual firms or industries within the cluster is often more significant for competitive advantage."* (Porter, 2008, p. 231)

In other words, it is not the size of the individual companies, but the range or spread of companies, which is relevant within a cluster. Other than that, horizontal and/or vertical relationships between companies contribute to the development and strengthening of a cluster. Based on these linkages, clusters result in synergies being created, i.e. specialized labor, tacit knowledge and innovation. Furthermore, all actors involved in a cluster are characterized by sharing the same factor conditions, like for instance resources and infrastructure (Ingstrup et al., 2009). Furthermore, Porter (2008) describes clusters' effect on competitiveness, in coherence with three broad assertions:

1. Clusters can increase the productivity of constituent companies or industries.
2. Clusters can increase their capacity for innovation and furthermore, the growth of productivity.
3. Clusters can stimulate new business formations that support innovation and expand the cluster.

Moreover, Porter (2008) highlights that clusters become more competitive because of continuous development and innovation. This can be achieved by the following:

- the intense rivalry between the participating companies

67

- start-ups from existing companies
- development of specialized products and services
- closeness to customers
- the link to advanced technological industries
- developing and spreading knowledge

The following section will explain the effect clusters can have on the actors within the cooperation.

## The Cluster's Effect on Its Participants

Porter (2008) points out the following effects that a cluster can have on its participants: 1) Increasing productivity, 2) Increasing capacity for innovation, and 3) Other general types of spillover effects. These effects are caused in part by being located in close proximity to one's customers and suppliers, thereby presenting a company with tangible benefits, such as reduced logistics costs, an enlarged pool of readily available skilled and educated labor, and a reduction/elimination of import/export complications and associated costs. Not only tangible, but also intangible benefits, such as closer and more cooperative relationships with business partners can be realized. These effects are however, also caused by operating in a transparent and competitive environment, where knowledge sharing is taking place (Porter, 2008). Therefore, for the individual company that is part of this environment, an incentive and pressure to develop is present. Some would view this pressure as negative (resistance to change), but for companies who are able to withstand this negative pressure, their presence inside the cluster will make them more attractive than those who are not present. This provides the company with a competitive advantage through increased customer attraction and retention. More specifically, Porter states that a cluster:

> "... may thus be defined as a system of interconnected firms and institutions, whose value as a whole is greater than the sum of its parts."
> (Porter, 2008, p. 229)

In other words, a common objective seems to exist for all companies that constitute a cluster: everybody gains from participating.

After this overview, the remaining part of this section will provide a closer look on how clusters and productivity are correlated.

## Access to Specialized Inputs and Employees

Porter (2008) points out that the decision of being inside or outside a cluster is an essential subject. The argument is that by being inside a cluster, the company can gain competitive advantages, e.g. through lower transaction costs, skilled workforce, a reduction in inventory, and a partial or complete elimination of import complications - all of which can lead to an increase in productivity. Porter (2008) states:

> *"Locating within a cluster can provide superior or lower-cost access to specialized inputs such as components, machinery, business services, and personnel, as compared to the alternatives – vertical integration, formal alliances with outside entities, or "importing" inputs from distant locations. (…) if competitive local suppliers are available."* (Porter, 2008, p. 230)

When focusing on the availability of a skilled workforce, which can indeed be a competitive advantage for the individual company, it would seem that costs associated with sourcing specialized employees are reduced. This can be seen by looking at the individual employee. After relocating to a cluster, he or she now has an opportunity as well as a reduced risk of having to relocate again for a new job. That is, once people have been sourced to the cluster, it is easier to keep them among the participating companies. The argument behind this statement is an increased ease of matching people to the right job, as well as the availability of many similar jobs in the cluster. Porter (2008) states:

> *"Where a cluster exists, the availability of specialized personnel, services, and components and the number of entities creating them usually far exceeds the levels at other locations, a distinct benefit, despite the greater competition."* (Porter, 2008, p. 232)

## Access to Information

To start out by quoting Porter, internal access to relevant information can be extended outside the company's four walls to the boundaries of the cluster. This provides the individual participant (either part of the triple helix – be that a company, knowledge institution or government body) with an advantage, which can assist in increasing productivity.

> *"Extensive market technical, and other specialized information accumulates within a cluster in firms and local institutions. This can be*

*accessed better or at lower cost from within the cluster, thus allowing firms to enhance productivity."* (Porter, 2008, p. 232)

As mentioned in the introduction of this literature review, the underlying reason for better access to know-how, at lower cost, is a build-up of trust and transparency through personal relationships, which are easier to maintain with companies and institutions, which are co-located within the cluster. Thus, it is not only sticky information, such as poor performance of a given participant, as mentioned earlier, but also relevant, significant information, which will be easily transferred between cluster participants. Porter (2008) gives a specific example of such shared information:

> "*Sophisticated buyers are often part of clusters, and other cluster participants often gain and share information about buyer needs.*" (Porter, 2008, p. 233)

## Complementing Each Other in the Cluster

Continuing the discussion about the resourcefulness and not the size of the participants (whether they are companies, knowledge institutions or public authorities), Porter (2008) argues that the span of relevant businesses in the cluster creates complementary effects. This can be realized in areas such as sourcing, marketing, technology and customer's efficiency, which will be shortly exemplified:

> "*The presence of a cluster also can enhance buying efficiency. Visiting buyers can see numerous firms in a single trip. The presence of multiple sources for a product or service in one location can also reduce perceived buying risk by offering buyers the potential to multisource or switch vendors if the need arises. Hong Kong thrives as a source of fashion apparel in part for this reason.*" (Porter, 2008, p. 234)

Just as good or superior performance of a cluster can attract business to the cluster, the reverse is also important to bear in mind, as there is a downside to this advantage. Porter (2008) states that:

> "*Bad performance by one part of the cluster can undermine the success of the others.*" (Porter, 2008, p. 233)

70

## Access to Institutions and Public Goods

A public good is a good, which is non-rivalrous and non-excludable in nature. It is a good that everybody has easy and costless access to, like a free radio signal. Using it, does not constrain others from using the same resource. The point that Porter (2008) makes about public goods in connection with clusters is therefore quite relevant, as he believes that a cluster can create public goods, which are then available to the cluster participants at decreased or lowered cost:

> *"Clusters make many inputs that would otherwise be costly into public or quasi-public goods. The ability to recruit employees trained in local programs, for example, eliminates or lowers the cost of internal training. Firms can often access benefits, such as specialized infrastructure or advice from experts in local institutions at very low cost."* (Porter, 2008, p. 234)

Notably, Porter (2008) describes how these public and quasi-public goods often are a result of private investments made inside the cluster. This could be in areas such as training programs as mentioned above, or infrastructure, quality centers etc. Regarding motivation behind the investments, Porter notes that:

> *"…such private investments are common because cluster participants perceive the potential for collective benefits."* (Porter, 2008, p. 234)

## Incentives and Performance Measurement

Porter (2008) argues that clusters improve incentives to achieve high productivity within companies. The reason is, as mentioned earlier, the competitive pressure from competitors, as well as peers in the cluster that are not direct competitors, but working in related industries, making external comparison straight-forward and transparent to members of the cluster. Furthermore, overall long-term goals following an investment in developing a local presence influence the interactions between members, also because of the transparency of interaction to other members. In other words, members or participants are aware that their actions are reflected back on them. The placement in the cluster is thereby a motivator for constructive interaction, as is building a positive reputation by superior internal and external performance.

## Summary of Porter's Cluster Theory

To summarize, the basic thoughts of Porter's theory are to look at companies and their contexts, in order to use these contexts as a tool to understand surrounding advantages or disadvantages, so competitive advantages in a global market context can be created. In other words, how to understand business conditions in a global spectrum, and how they are different from each other. One of the important things he states is the potential for productivity advantages to be gained by participating in a cluster. Porter (2008) states the following, which holds true for domestic as well as foreign companies, as long as the individual company makes a permanent investment to achieve a significant, local presence:

> *"As has been noted, many of these productivity advantages of clusters involve location-specific public goods or benefits that depend on physical proximity, face-to-face contact, close and ongoing relationships, and "insider" access to information. The benefits of cluster membership can thus be difficult if not impossible to access unless firms participate actively, with a significant local presence."* (Porter, 2008, p. 236)

For a better understanding of Porter's theory, he contributed to theorizing about clustering with his diamond shaped model called: *Sources of Locational Competitive Advantage* (Porter, 2008). The model is relevant, because it highlights how competitiveness on a nation level can be improved, among others through cluster activity. In the following section, Porter's *Sources of Locational Competitive Advantage* will therefore be presented and examined, putting focus on the government's role and motivation in clusters, as successful clusters can help for instance nations, states, metropolitan areas and cities to gain competitive advantages in the increasingly globalized marketplace.

## Sources of Locational Competitive Advantage

From Porter's (2008) view, clustering cannot be understood only by competition and the influence of location in the global economy. As a result of this, he created a model *Sources of Locational Competitive Advantage* that gives an understanding of location and competition. This model proposes not only a question of cost minimization or economies of scale, but also extendedly other relevant factors.

Competition is determined to be *"dynamic and rests on innovations and the search for strategic differences"* (Porter, 1998, p. 209). Porter (1998) emphasizes that it is important to have close linkages with your buyers, suppliers and other institutions. These will then contribute to efficiency and product innovations in close cooperation. Furthermore, he states that location contributes to productivity, and that any industry can use advanced technology to be more productive and effective, but it all depends on how they compete, if companies wants to be successful. Through his studies, he created the model, known as *Sources of Locational Competitive Advantages*, which is compounded of four dimensions, as illustrated beneath in Figure 3.1.

The boxes in the diamond describe what leads to a comparative advantage. Porter's *Sources of Locational Competitive Advantages* uses four determinants which are *factor conditions, demand conditions, firm strategy, structure and rivalry* and *related and supporting industries*. For a better understanding of the model, the four dimensions will be described in the following.

*1. Factor Input Conditions*

- Factor (input) quantity and cost:
  *Natural resources, Human resources, Capital resources, Physical infrastructure, Administrative infrastructure, Information infrastructure, Scientific and technological infrastructure*
- Factor quality
- Factor specialization

*2. Demand Conditions*

- Sophisticated and demanding local customer(s)
- Customer needs that anticipate those elsewhere
- Unusual local demand in specialized segments that can be served globally

*3. Related and Supporting Industries*

- Presence of capable, locally-based suppliers
- Presence of competitive related industries

*4. Firm Strategy Structure and Rivalry*

- A local context that encourages appropriate forms of investment and sustained upgrading

- Vigorous competition among locally-based rivals

*Figure 3.1: Sources of Locational Competitive Advantages*

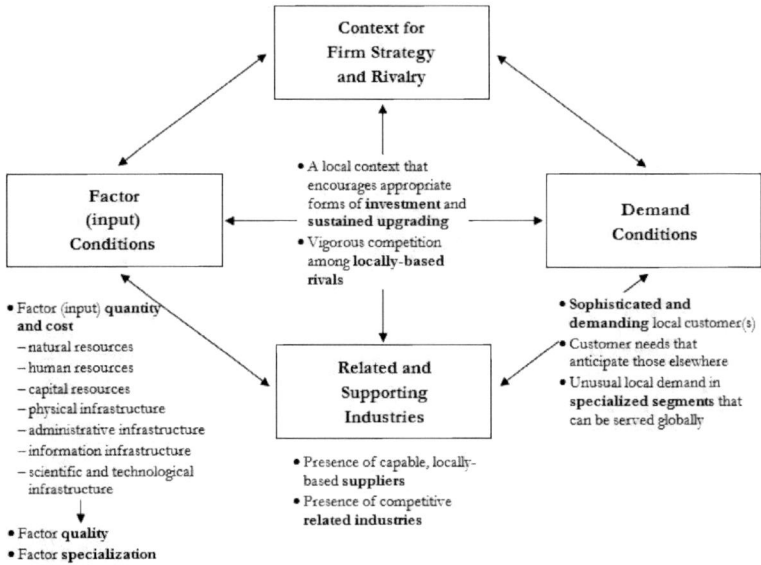

```
                        ┌─────────────────┐
                        │   Context for   │
                        │  Firm Strategy  │
                        │   and Rivalry   │
                        └─────────────────┘
```

• A local context that
encourages appropriate
forms of **investment** and
**sustained upgrading**
• Vigorous competition
among **locally-based
rivals**

```
┌──────────────┐                              ┌──────────────┐
│   Factor     │                              │    Demand    │
│   (input)    │                              │  Conditions  │
│  Conditions  │                              │              │
└──────────────┘                              └──────────────┘
```

• Factor (input) **quantity**
  **and cost**
  – natural resources
  – human resources
  – capital resources
  – physical infrastructure
  – administrative infrastructure
  – information infrastructure
  – scientific and technological
    infrastructure
• Factor **quality**
• Factor **specialization**

```
                        ┌─────────────────┐
                        │   Related and   │
                        │   Supporting    │
                        │   Industries    │
                        └─────────────────┘
```

• Presence of capable, locally-
  based **suppliers**
• Presence of competitive
  **related industries**

• **Sophisticated and
  demanding** local customer(s)
• Customer needs that
  anticipate those elsewhere
• Unusual local demand in
  **specialized segments** that
  can be served globally

Source: Porter (2008, p. 227)

Furthermore, in coherence to the model, Porter describes the role of government in clustering.

## The Role of Government

The government's role is to encourage and push companies to perform better, and raise their level of performance and through this, raise their level of competitiveness. Furthermore, it is important for a government to stimulate the demand for advanced products. This will help industries to innovate and develop competitiveness. Moreover, government bodies can stimulate innovation in companies, through symbolic, cooperative/joint projects. Governments can only succeed in pushing companies to perform better, if they work in tandem with the conditions stated in Porter's *Sources of Locational Competitive Advantages* (Porter, 2008).

When mentioning clustering and localization, Porter's *Sources of Locational Competitive Advantages* provides a platform for discussing which advantages and disadvantages are available in the chosen geographical area. This is of great importance for companies when they are considering different localizations and how to select between these. For instance, is it important that production costs are low? That skilled workforce is available nearby, including access to graduates? That the suppliers are placed nearby? Is it important to be located in the same geographical area as the actors within the entire value chain? Or is it merely important to be located close to suppliers with capable resources? These questions are some of the many questions that companies that consider locating within a cluster need to ask themselves. Using Porter's *Sources of Locational Competitive Advantages* as a framework can provide some of the answers that can be helpful in this decision-making process.

## Location Specific Advantages

Companies considering interaction on a global scale will need to apply a framework for understanding internal coherences between isolated company activities. This is needed to comprehend changes within the company as a unified whole, due to the changes in company operations, as a result of transactions made on a global scale. An example of such a framework was provided by Dunning in 1991, proposing his eclectic paradigm, the OLI model (Dunning, 1993, pp. 76-85). OLI stands for: *Ownership specific advantages*, *Location specific advantages* and *Internalization specific advantages*.

In regard to this chapter's research of cluster activity in Southern India, the aspects of *Ownership-* and *Internalization- specific advantages* have been left out. This has been done to be able to focus on localization specific advantages, due to its coherency with aspects of localization theory, in correlation to cluster theory.

The term *Location specific advantages* (Dunning, 1993, p. 77), relates to advantages gained by being located in the specific area that the company is located in. Some examples of these kinds of advantages could be easy access to certain kinds of raw materials, low wages, skilled labor, access to knowledge, shipping advantages to company customers, market structure, tax benefits in comparison to the native country of the company, legal aspects, cultural aspects like work ethics etc.

### Infrastructure

The infrastructural aspect of localization is essential for almost any company. It is obvious that if companies are not able to move their goods from point A to point B in an acceptable period of time, according to their customers' needs, they are simply not going to be successful as a contractor. This is the reason why companies place great importance in being located in close proximity to a functional infrastructural network, in accordance with their own needs, as well as their customers'.

When involved in global trade, for instance as a manufacturer within the clothing industry, it is most likely that being located in proximity to a harbor will be beneficial to the company, in order to ship out large quantities of goods. For other industries, it will be important to be located in proximity to an airport, for instance within the courier industry, in order to speed up time of transportation. But not only transportation possibilities are relevant, when looking at a certain area's infrastructural network. Also, the possibility for modern communication and the opportunity to acquire sufficient amounts of electricity to maintain the company's operational level are important factors, when assessing an area's infrastructural network level. It is therefore clear that today's technologically based companies are in need of modern technological opportunities, to stay in contact with customers and suppliers.

Technological services provided by energy suppliers, mobile phone operators and internet operators are needed when doing business in a modern world. It is therefore essential that these service opportunities are present in a well-functioning infrastructural network. Second to their presence in the given area of localization, it is also important that the costs of these services are competitive on a comparative level. Costs of acquiring these services can consequently either facilitate localization or make localization in the given area too costly in the long run.

## Access to Raw Materials and Semi-Manufactured Goods

Another important factor with regard to localization of company operations is the accessibility to raw materials and semi-manufactured goods. The reason why this is important is that easy accessibility to these kinds of materials will increase the company's comparative competition level, if the company is located within the manufacturing business. Furthermore, being located in an area in close proximity to manufacturers of raw materials and semi-manufactured goods will secure the company's position to be able to deliver to customers on time, due to a reduction in order time as a unified whole.

## Access to Skilled Labor

An additional essential factor with regard to localization is the access to skilled labor. This is essential, whether the company is in need of skilled workers in term of craftsmen, or in terms of workers with a higher degree of specialization or education. As a result of this, localization can be driven by the requirement for specific needs for a certain type of know how. Access to this knowledge is consequently essential for companies to be able to evolve. For instance, a company's need for highly educated workers can be met by being located in an area where knowledge institutions like technical schools, colleges and universities are present. As a result of a location in such an area, a company's accessibility to attract qualified labor will often improve due to the area's knowledge of the company. Furthermore, location in close proximity to knowledge institutions will often result in collaboration between the company and a given knowledge institution, for example on tasks like research projects.

## Macro-Economic Factors

Furthermore, aspects like a well developed market structure in the area of location will assist companies in doing trade in a more efficient way. In addition to this, a well developed market structure is often facilitated by governmental arrangements like for instance a more gentle tax level, in comparison to the native country of the company. Additionally, a cultural aspect like better work ethics in a given area can be perceived as a localization advantage, due to a more productive work force.

# Reflection on Porter and Dunning's Theories

There are many similarities to be discovered, when comparing the theories described by Porter and Dunning. Especially, when comparing Dunning's (1993) location specific advantages with Porter's (2008) overall competitive advantages of clusters. It is important to remember that the theories from both authors are descriptive, but not particularly normative. This is important, because these years' economies and markets change at a rapid pace. What is beneficial for the company today might not be so tomorrow. It is therefore of great importance to always be looking to the market to notice changes in real time, so that it is possible to adjust in time, to achieve company objectives. An overview of possible advantages and disadvantages, discussed in previous sections, are shown in Table 3.1.

*Table 3.1: Possible (Dis)Advantages of Participating in a Cluster*

| Productivity gains when participating in a cluster | Possible competitive/ cost advantages | Possible disadvantages |
|---|---|---|
| Employees | Lower costs associated with sourcing within the cluster | Retention: Easier for employees to shop around for similar job inside cluster |
| Specialized inputs | Competitive cost advantage Lower transaction costs Reduction in inventory (through supply chain physically located in the cluster) Reduced or eliminated import complications (similar to working inside EU) | |
| Access to information | Better access or at lower cost – easily transferred between cluster participants Reputation build-up through word-of mouth inside cluster | Sticky information – poor performance is equally fast transferred |
| Complementing each other in the cluster | Synergy in business processes. E.g. sourcing, marketing, technology, customers' efficiency. | Time consumption (pragmatism) and interdependence between participants |
| Institutions and public goods | Lower cost of (internal) training of workforce through local programs | |
| Incentives and performance measurement | External (in cluster) comparison to other companies Incentive for continuous improvement in productivity caused by transparent competition Motivation for constructive interaction (with companies in related industries) | Increased competition |

Source: Own compilation, based on Porter (2008) and Dunning (1993)

## Methodology

The overall objective with this field study is to investigate cluster activity in Southern India. This research has been undertaken as an exploratory study with an effectuation approach (Andersen, 2005), which in this case means that it has been carried out with the objective to study given companies' ways of thinking localization and clustering in general. Furthermore, it also means that the study has been undertaken as a project of practical exercise, where students have carried out investigative reporting by seeking out relevant companies in Southern India. Subsequently, it meant traveling to India to interview these companies, in contrast to solely conducting desk-research. In addition to this, it should be emphasized that desk research has been carried out in preparation for the visits to the companies in question. This has been done with regard to gathering initial background knowledge about the respective companies, to enable a more thorough study.

As preparation for the field study, a literature review was made in order to create an understanding of the topic 'Clusters in Southern India'. This literature review consisted of findings from relevant secondary data sources, such as academic articles, books, web pages, etc., which deal with clusters and localization theory. Because the visited companies need to retain their anonymity, their web pages are not referred to, nor are they in the list of references. Furthermore, this study also consists of primary data that have been collected from four companies, which all are located in Bangalore and Chennai in Southern India.

These primary data where obtained via semi-structured interviews with key representatives from the visited companies. These representatives were either Danish or Indian. Each interview was structured according to an interview guide, which was sent to the companies beforehand. This procedure was chosen in order to give the company the opportunity to become familiar with our questions and prepare qualified answers (Heldbjerg, 2006). It was also done with regard to the language barrier, since both parties only regard English as their second language. This means that both parties might not be able to make themselves as fully understandable as in their respective native languages.

The general procedure during the visits to the companies started with an introduction to the company and their activities followed by a Q&A session based on the interview guides and follow-up questions to the presentation given. The visits ended with a tour around the company facility.

This study represents a broad range of industries, ranging from the textile industry to the energy industry. The study therefore provides an overview of how companies from different industries choose their location: What benefits did they expect – which benefits were realized?

## Empirical Findings

In the following company descriptions and analyses, sources are primarily from annual reports, as well as from the conducted interviews. The chosen companies will not be mentioned by name, as they desire to remain anonymous. As a consequence, specific sources are not listed.

## Company Descriptions

Based on the purpose and the research question of this chapter, a short presentation of the four visited companies will follow in this section. To oblige with the promises of anonymity, these four are called A, B, C and D.

### Company A

Company A is an Indian company located in the textile industry, which deals with production of clothes. The company was previously located in Mumbai, but has for the last five years been settled in Bangalore. The company has approximately 4-500 employees at this location, from where they serve customers in India, as well as in Europe and USA. Primary customers include large international fashion companies, as well as large retail chains of discount department stores. The company's overall capacity of production is 100,000 units of clothing a month.

### Company B

Company B is a Danish manufacturer within the wind turbine industry. This company operates on a global scale, and has subsidiaries located on each continent, from where it can service its customers. Their Indian headquarters is located in Chennai close to their suppliers, which makes the delivery time on raw materials short and uncomplicated. These suppliers are divided into classes, based on importance of raw materials, being classified as class A, B, C etc. Company B services both private customers, as well as public energy companies on a global base. The number of employees is roughly 20,000 worldwide, while only 600 of them are employed in India at 7 different locations.

### Company C

Company C is a worldwide supplier of pump solutions, mainly circulator and centrifugal pumps. The company employs approximately 17,000 employees worldwide. They are the world's largest supplier with regards to circulator pumps, with a market share above 50 percent of the global market. This company produces altogether over 16 million units annually, which makes it world leader within the pump industry. This specific company has a portfolio of activities that includes more than 80 companies in 45 countries, of which 14 have local production facilities. Company C's primary customers are large international companies. Their Indian headquarter are located in Chennai, where activities such as production, sales and service operations are taking place. Their subsidiaries in India, which mainly focus on sales, are among others located in Delhi, Bangalore and Mumbai.

## Company D

Company D is a Danish company in the cement and mineral industry, which operates on a global scale. This company has a local presence in more than 40 countries, with major project centers in Denmark, USA and India. The company employs about 9,000 people worldwide, including about 1,650 spread out over different locations in India. When it comes to customers, they can be defined as local, regional and even global cement producing companies. Capacity has decreased markedly since 2008. At the time, the company exported about 150 million tons of cement, while in 2009 it was only about 40-50 million tons. In both cases, the Chinese market was not included.

## Expected and Experienced Advantages/Disadvantages

### Company A

*Incentives for Choice of Location.* The primary reason why company A moved its location to Bangalore five years ago was the possibility of reducing their production costs radically, especially regarding labor and electricity costs. For instance, wage regulations differ from state to state in India, e.g. on minimum salary. When comparing labor laws in Mumbai with labor laws in Bangalore, the company is able to save about 3,000 rupees per employee per month, by re-locating itself to Bangalore. Furthermore, land prices in the Bangalore area were lower than in other potential locations, which also helped lowering the overall costs for the company.

Another important reason for the choice of this specific location in Bangalore was to place themselves next to their competitors. The purpose of this was to bring the company closer to its competitor's customers, in order to have the opportunity to offer its products to new potential customers – i.e. taking customers from competitors. By doing this, it would prove itself to be easier for the customer to get an overview of the possibilities on the market, since they are able to obtain a wider range of options in one limited geographic area. Furthermore, locating oneself near competitive companies creates the opportunity of attracting skilled labor from these competitors if or when needed, as pointed out by Porter (2008).

Another advantage that company A expected from locating itself within a geographically limited area of companies in Bangalore was to take advantage of the similar prevailing production method in this area. The culture of using the *operator paced line production* (Miltenburg, 2005) is the most common production method in Bangalore, where approximately 80 percent of all clothing manufacturers use this method of production.

This gives the company the advantage of recruiting employees from their competitors, which thereby reduces training costs. Company A, therefore, gained from the rivalry within the textile industry, because employees shop around for better terms and salary, simultaneously improving the skills of the workforce within the cluster, as previously discussed by Porter (2008). Moreover, employees want to earn more, so they specialize in one thing, because they are paid in a piecework reward system. For employees, it means that they can freely move between companies, without much trouble.

Expected disadvantages that follow the decision of relocating would be the longer distance to suppliers, which means that the time of delivery on raw materials becomes a prolonged process. Also, costs of transportation regarding these raw materials will either be increased or sustained at the same level. However, when looking at logistics costs, it can be observed that these costs are very low in India, and in perspective to the total cost of goods therefore rather unimportant to focus on. In general, the expectations for this relocation were to obtain significant cost reductions.

*Current Situation.* The expectations company A had before relocating to Bangalore were after some time almost all met. In some cases, it took a longer period of time to adapt, for instance to familiarize themselves with new rules, as they vary from state to state. In this case, it required the company to acquaint itself with existing (labor) laws in the area, which took the company between one and one and a half years before things became more stable. The company did not expect the process to take that amount of time, but in the long term, it had no great effect on the decision on relocation.

## Company B

*Incentives for Choice of Location.* Company B's choice of locating itself in Chennai was mainly based upon exploiting the opportunity of the lucrative wind conditions in this specific part of India. The Indian government has played an active role in the promotion of sustainable energy solutions by mapping wind conditions throughout India. This active role played by the Indian government has been one of the major reasons for company B locating in Chennai. Another important advantage of this location is that the harbor is close by, which reduces transportation time with regard to getting parts from around the world, and at the same time reduces the costs of shipping.

The A-class suppliers of this company are located in Chennai. Given that a key-supplier and partner are located within the same area, often promotes greater cooperation, especially within research and development of products, as indicated by Porter (2008). To be located in close proximity to its suppliers increases the company's expectations of better and easier ways of cooperation. Moreover, the company has a selected number of specialized skilled personnel stationed at their suppliers, to make sure that products meet the given standards.

In addition, the company seeks to exploit advantages of their location close to knowledge institutions, such as universities, by cooperating with students, who get the opportunity to resolve various projects that are essential for developing innovative contributions to new standards.

*Current Situation.* Nearly all expectations that company B had before entering Chennai were met. The company's desire to engage in closer cooperation with knowledge institutions such as universities, led to many positive experiences. The student's contributions to projects initiated by the company gives the advantage of being dynamic and always at the front of new and innovative solutions. Beyond that, the company found that being located closely to these institutions makes it easier to collaborate and gives the company greater advantages than anticipated.

After locating in Chennai, Company B realized that not only knowledge institutions and suppliers were important to cooperate with. Driven by an industry-wide need to change laws, Company B joined a council with other members of the energy cluster, including competitors, where common interests are discussed, and joint lobbying efforts towards lawmakers are agreed upon.

## Company C

*Incentives for Choice of Location.* Company C strongly believes that local presence is an important factor with respect to penetrating the local market. Local presence was the major reason for locating in India – with more than just sales operations. Therefore, they have warehousing, manufacturing and sales altogether placed in Chennai, including the vast majority of management. For the same reason, company C has 19 key account managers placed in local offices all over India, dealing with local regional customers.

When choosing Chennai over other possible locations in India, there were three main decisive factors: *Superior work-culture* based on access to highly educated employees from local universities in Chennai, as well as the already existing pool of employees working in related industries; *optimal infrastructure* - in the form of close proximity to both harbor and airport; and lastly the *absence of competitors* in the area. The first factor fits well with Porter's theory about cluster benefits, which indicates that locating within a cluster will give easier access to highly skilled and trained labor at reduced cost, mainly because of two factors: firstly, retention of employees within the cluster, creating a joint pool of employees that change between cluster participants, and secondly the presence of knowledge institutions who facilitate the training and education of employees.

To elaborate on this last factor, company C does not have competitors, which deliver the same quality and product standards as they do. There are numerous companies that provide a similar product and substitutes, but they are not as effective as company C´s products. The company's main concern in India is its experiences with copy-manufacturers on a very widespread scale. Legislation wise, it is a long and tiresome effort to deal with this problem. The fact that these copycats exist in the same geographical area means that the company is in need of continuous development and innovation of its products, as a response to competition.

When company C was choosing its specific location in India, the government and authorities in Chennai were facilitating a new industrial area. This is also one of the major reasons why company C is located in Chennai today. The fact that land was very expensive in India and hard to acquire, made it easier for the company to take this decision, now that the government opened a great opportunity for new businesses.

*Current Situation.* Company C focuses on process innovation (as opposed to product innovation), often regarded as an incremental innovation, and focuses on hiring newly educated graduates, who are then trained internally to suit the company's specific needs. With respect to their widely spread sales network in India, company C makes an effort to be an active partner, when customers, whether existing or potential, need new innovative solutions in connection with larger industrial setups requiring an integrated pump solution. An example of this is wastewater treatment plants.

## Company D

*Incentives for Choice of Location.* Company D is a Danish based company in the cement and mineral industry. They chose to set up in India, because of the growing demand in the Asian market for building equipment and machines to extract raw materials for the growing demand for cement. Furthermore, setting up in India has created a sustainable cost reduction in comparison to production costs in Denmark. This cost reduction constitutes a reduction of up to 80 percent of manufacturing prices in comparison to Denmark, and was a consideration before moving.

India was chosen over China, because this country was of greater potential in the long run. Chennai was chosen as a location, due to the findings of a task group. This task group made their decision based on a scoring-card, which compared advantages and disadvantages of different areas. According to the CEO of Indian operations, they could have located their headquarter anywhere in India, it would not had made any difference. In terms of locating operations in an area with skilled workers, craftsmen as well as higher educated personal, the location in Chennai was considered to be of good potential. Especially since this company seeks to have permanent staff as well as part-time labor, when needed.

They could have chosen to be located anywhere in India, for the reason that skilled labor is to be obtained anywhere in India at present time, and skilled labor are willing to move within India, as well as outside India for a better job. By choosing Chennai as location for their operations in India, the company estimated that easy access to the harbor would be another great advantage for them. Another argument for their location choice was Chennai's infrastructure, which was of great importance, because of a better composition due to reduced travel time between meetings with business partners. For the same reason, company D did not regard location in Bangalore or Mumbai, for example, to be an equally good opportunity.

*Current Situation.* The advantages of being located in Chennai did almost meet their expectations. However, one difficulty is still faced with regard to retaining skilled workers, because these tend to shop around for a better job. This is a challenge because training new workers can be a costly affair for companies.

# Discussion

Based on the empirical findings, it became clear that companies benefit from being located in the same geographical area as their suppliers and/or customers, in comparison with Porter (2008) and his reflections on factor conditions. The benefits from being located in a cluster are to a great extent similar to the localization advantages stated by Dunning (1993).

Clustering is not that widespread in India, or at least knowledge about being present in clusters. This is among other things caused by the fact that industrial development is rather limited compared to the western world. For example, triple helix cooperation (Etzkowitz and Leydesdorff, 2000) is almost none existing in India, and triple helix actors are normally those which are related to dynamic cooperation and innovation inside clusters.

However, cluster activities do to some extend contribute to improvements in the participating companies. Due to competition and internal rivalry in the cluster, company A, for example, is forced to be innovative and effective in their way of producing, otherwise related and supporting industries will take over their market position. In this way, the cluster puts an extra pressure on participating companies; a pressure they otherwise would not have noticed or not as intense. The empirical findings from the four companies will be placed in a matrix of own compilation, in accordance to each company's degree of localization and clustering.

## Cluster Location Matrix

Based on the company descriptions and analyses, it was deemed appropriate to create a matrix to visualize how the importance of location of business activities and cluster development are connected. First, a thorough explanation of the matrix will be presented, which includes descriptions of the values on the axes, as well as the types of companies in the respective quadrants. The explanation will be followed by a reflection on the case companies, based on the types of companies, the conducted desk research, and the experienced characteristics during the four company visits in India.

## Defining the Axes

*Horizontal Axis.* On the horizontal axis, the scale ranges from low to high development of clustering. This implies not only the development or maturation of the given cluster, but also the level of participation of the individual company. Thus, which end of the scale a company is placed in is strongly connected to its willingness to participate. One cannot realize and reap benefits, if one is not aware of them; this means that awareness is a critical factor for cluster development and participation; awareness of the cluster, its activities and the potential benefits to be gained by active participation. Following awareness is willingness to collaborate with other actors outside the company e.g. other companies, knowledge institutions, and government bodies. Willingness as well as unwillingness to collaborate can manifest itself in general guidelines or policies from top management, or in the case of a strongly decentralized organization, in the opinion of local management. A good example of this was experienced during the interview with company D, where the CEO of the Indian office said: *"We only cooperate with government bodies if we really have to"*.

*Vertical Axis*. On the vertical axis, the scale is more clearly dichotomous: *Core* or *Peripheral*. In this context, core and peripheral relates to whether the decision to locate in a specific area was critical to core business activities. If location was not important to a specific company, placement in the matrix would be in the peripheral end of the vertical axis.

## Defining Quadrants and Placing Company A-D

In Figure 3.2, the matrix as described above is illustrated. Accordingly, the type of the companies placed in each of the four quadrants will be described and discussed.

*Figure 3.2: Location- vs. Development-Matrix for Company A, B, C and D*

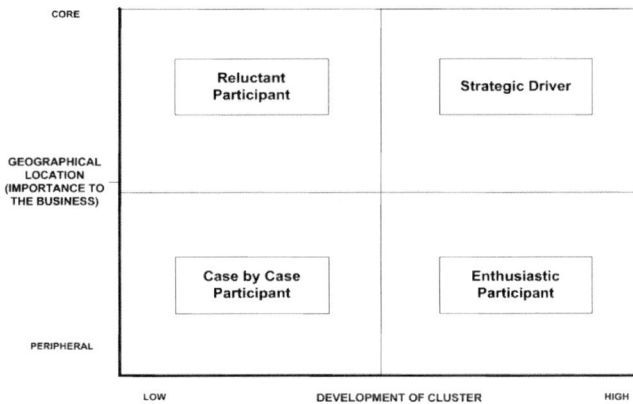

Source: Own compilation

*Case by Case Participant – Company D*. Location is not important to core business activities. In other words, for this type of company, specific

87

geographical location is not critical. Furthermore, if a cluster is present in the geographical area, benefits of participation are either not identified, or not deemed relevant to the business from a cost-benefit point of view.

For this company D, specific geographical location was not important to core business activities. Likewise, awareness of the cluster and its activities were very low. The few realized potential benefits of participating actively in the cluster were not deemed worth the effort. Participation in cluster activities was therefore based solely on occasional need-to cases, such as government policy.

*Reluctant Participant – Company B.* Location is critical to core business activities. This entails great importance to geographical location of the business, more specifically factor inputs: e.g. in form of closeness to market, knowledge institutions, specialized workforce, infrastructure hubs etc. Furthermore, if a cluster is present in the geographical area, benefits of participation are either not identified, or not deemed relevant to the business from a cost-benefit point of view.

For this company B, specific geographical location is critical to core business activities. But on the other hand, cluster activities, if present, are not identified or of very low character. Participating in cluster activities is only occasional.

*Enthusiastic Participant – Company C.* Location is not important to core business activities. In other words, for this type of company, specific geographical location is not critical. However, while geographical location as such is not critical to core business activities, presence inside a cluster is realized to have potential benefits. This type of company is therefore an active participant in cluster activities, motivated by limited parts of cluster benefits, such as access to a specialized workforce and access to information.

Location for company C is not crucial for core business activities, due to the fact that company C could have placed their headquarter anywhere in India. In contrast to location, company C participates in cluster activities, and rates it as a motivator to gain benefits from clustering. For example access to specialized workforce and knowledge.

*Strategic Driver – Company A.* As for the reluctant participant, location is critical to core business activities. This entails great importance to geographical location of the business, more specifically factor inputs: e.g. in form of closeness to market, knowledge institutions, specialized workforce, infrastructure hubs etc. This type of company is both aware of location benefits as well as cluster benefits, before locating in the area.

To company A, location is a key factor to business activities, and location advantages and factor inputs are important to production and effectiveness of the production. In addition to location, clustering is of high priority to company A, and they have sought out the location because of the advantages and cluster benefits. All four companies are positioned in Figure 3.3.

*Figure 3.3: Case Companies Positioned in the Location- vs. Development-Matrix*

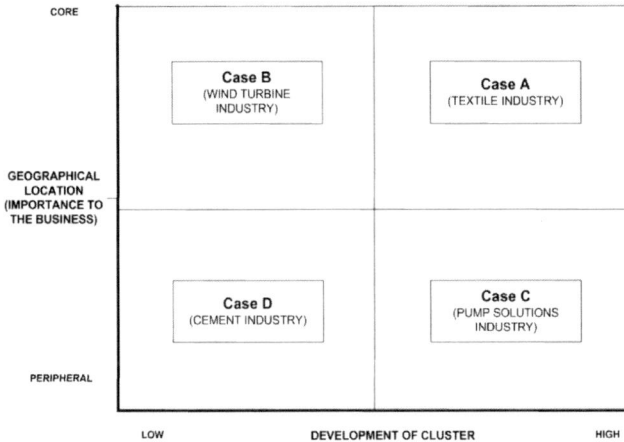

Source: Own compilation

To sum up, all four companies have been illustrated and placed in the matrix. When looking at the matrix, it is clear that for some companies, location is crucial to their existence. Furthermore, it shows that location is a strategic and deliberate choice for some of these investigated companies. An example is company A, which has moved to a location in another region, due to the fact that production cost were lower there, and moreover because of the working culture in exactly that area. These were the major reasons for their relocation to Bangalore. To other companies, location is not critical to their core activities. Some companies could be located anywhere in India, and still have a successful business. For Danish companies considering moving to India, it is important to make strategic location choices and be aware of the advantages and disadvantages of the specific areas.

89

# Conclusion

The purpose of this chapter was to identify and portray cluster activity in Southern India, and to discuss how companies located in this particular area could benefit from their location. The empirical study done answered the research question and contributed with a perspective on what to consider before entering India, with regard to location and clustering.

After conducting interviews with four different companies, both Danish and Indian, it appeared that these were not familiar with the term cluster. However, our study revealed that some of these companies were actually located in a cluster, which furthermore had a decisive impact on their business operation, as well as their business strategy. This was illustrated in Figure 3.2 and 3.3, *Location- vs. development-matrix for company A-D*, where it among others was shown that both company A and C are located in a cluster. For these two companies, the importance of finding the right location proved to be significant, while the remaining two companies believed location to be of less significance. As a result of this, they should be able to position themselves relatively randomly in India. This is due to their belief that a selection of a given location would not specifically contribute with any significant benefits on its own. The conclusion here is that even though some of these companies did not consider themselves as being part of a cluster, this study showed otherwise.

This study furthermore revealed different factors that influenced the choice of location. These factors were for instance infrastructural network conditions, such as distances to harbor or airport facilities, the accessibility of skilled labor in the area, suppliers' location, labor laws with particular influence on wages, competitors' position, land prices, different working cultures from state to state, and government allocation of an industrial area. These factors had different levels of importance for each company, where some had more relevance than others. These factors are all mentioned and described by Porter (2008), including the *Sources of Locational Competitive Advantage*, which can help Danish companies by providing an overview of the different factors in relation to clustering.

Furthermore, Danish companies should be advised to take Dunning's theory (1993) of *Location specific advantages* into consideration when choosing to locate in Southern India. With respect to this, it must be emphasized that it is of great importance that companies take into consideration the level of value creation the specific area of chosen localization can contribute with to the overall operation of the company.

Depending on which industry companies are located in, it can be beneficial to explore ways of clustering in India. The individual company has to consider if the chosen location is appropriate and necessary for its survival and further development, more so if a successful business depends on the facilitation of cluster activities. As a result of this, it should be stressed that localization in Southern India and participating in cluster activities should only be commenced if these activities will contribute to overall value creation, with regard to the company's output as a unified whole. However, if this is conceived to be the case, companies can experience great advantages from being located in Southern India.

# CHAPTER 4

# Relationship Management

*Nicolai Sebastian Bisgaard, Stine Dreier, Jeppe Bo Käehne, Frank Mikkelsberg, Stine Holm Sparwath, Jens Kallesøe Sørensen.*

## Abstract

*The purpose of this chapter is to describe and lay down guidelines for which issues to be aware of when doing business in India. India is a multicultural society in which relationships and trust are regarded as the main drivers for establishing a successful business. When entering a business relationship, it is therefore of great importance to be aware of cultural factors, environmental factors and factors affecting relationship management.*

## Introduction

The diversity of Indian culture will in many ways affect any given relationship with a Western country. Not only is there a cross-cultural issue between Indian and Western culture, there are even more complex cross-cultural issues between different regions within India itself. This scenario calls for the utmost focus on cultural issues when Western companies interact with Indian companies and vice versa. As such, these cultural differences should be taken into consideration in every aspect of the company's value chain. When this issue is considered alongside the cultural dimensions of House et al. (2004), a framework for working with cultural differences is drawn. These theoretical considerations, which are built on empirical data, have to be implemented in the business' supply chain to have any positive effect on the cross-cultural relationship. If this is successfully accomplished, it comes to function as a cultural foundation on which a business can create value in a cross-cultural perspective.

In continuation of the above, it would be obvious to question how these cross-cultural differences affect specific stages in the supply chain. To describe these implications in detail, this chapter finds it most appropriate to consider the relationship between Indian companies and their suppliers. This provides the opportunity to make a thorough qualitative analysis of the cross-cultural factors to be considered when relational actions are being made among Indian and Western companies. In order to give a thorough analysis of the customer relationship, this chapter has decided to focus on key account suppliers. This specific focus reflects the aspiration to find specific cultural differences that affect the relationship between Indian and Western companies based on the conclusions from the field study.

## Research Questions

The aim of this chapter is to get an understanding of the issues that impact the way of doing business in India. More specifically, this chapter will give an understanding of how relationship management is carried out in India between companies and their key account suppliers. Key account suppliers are defined as important suppliers whom companies rely on to obtain their strategic goals. This leads to the following overall research question:

> *"How is relationship management carried out in India between companies and their key account suppliers?"*

This is divided further into four sub-questions:

- **Research Question 1**
  Which cultural issues impact the way of doing business in India?

- **Research Question 2**
  Which environmental factors impact Indian business? (in terms of political, economical, social, technological and legal factors)

- **Research Question 3**
  What do companies have to consider with respect to cultural and environmental factors?

- **Research Question 4**
  How is relationship management used in an Indian context?

## Methodology

The preparation for this chapter took place in advance of the Indian fieldtrip. This was done to create a theoretical framework in order to understand and enlighten key factors regarding relationship management in a more broad perspective. The theoretical research consisted of relevant literature and articles. Since a more narrow perspective is needed to carry out thorough research, this chapter will try to cover the following specific problem: "How is relationship management carried out in India between companies and their key account suppliers?"

After reviewing the literature, a semi structured questionnaire guide was conducted to carry out the question sessions in India. The questionnaire guide was handed out to the companies in advance to insure they were prepared to answer the questions properly. During the sessions at the visited companies, the questions from the questionnaire guide were further elaborated on until the necessary level of data could be extracted.

The relatively broad range of companies visited should as a whole represent different perspectives on how relationship management is carried out in India. In continuation of this, it is important to mention that the composition of the visited companies varied in size, age, represented time in India, technology level, country of origin and the degree of collaboration with the western world. Industry-wise, the companies spanned from consultancy agencies to warehousing with service to entire production lines.

In all of the companies visited, top-level leaders who knew a lot about the entire company and the society surrounding the business were interviewed. All of the companies gave a great introduction to their company. After the presentation, there was the opportunity to ask the prepared questions if these were not answered in the presentation. In some of the sessions, all groups (relationship, clusters, outsourcing, and corporate social responsibility) were represented, while in other visits only the relationship management group was present. The latter resulted in more informal talks. This gave an idea of Indian culture in a more practical matter.

The research questions do not only focus on characteristics of the Indian market and do not attempt to compare this with Western markets. This chapter has the purpose to provide inspiration and guidelines. It will be up to the reader to interpret these guidelines from the study to their specific needs in a Western context. Thus, the focus is on Indian characteristics. Some of the interviewed informants were aware of Danish culture, due to the company's Danish origin. In this case, it was possible to discuss differences between Indian and Danish culture.

# Literature Review

This section explains which theoretical viewpoints will be used further in the present chapter. At first, this chapter will focus on Indian culture, leading to the environment in which it unfolds. In this sense, the next step is to be more specifically focused on how relationships in these environments are formed.

## Indian Culture

The introductory difficulties that emerge when working with culture are first and foremost how to define this extensive phenomenon. There are many theorists who deal with the subject culture, which obviously results in many different definitions of culture. These definitions and perceptions can serve as a frame when working with this topic. Thus, the first stage is to find a general definition of culture to provide a basis. Schein (1984) is one of the most prominent theorists in the field of organizational culture. He has formulated the following definition of culture:

> "*A pattern of shared basic assumptions that the group learned as it solved its problems of external adaptation and internal integration, that has worked well enough to be considered valid and therefore, to be taught to new members as the correct way to perceive, think, and feel in relation to those problems.*" (Schein, 1984)

This wide definition will be the starting point for any further work on culture.

To examine the cultural values of the Indian nation, cf. research question 1, we will make use of the acknowledged GLOBE framework. GLOBE, 'Global Leadership and Organizational Behavior Effectiveness Research Program', is a research program that House et al. (2004) conducted, resulting in an empirically-based theory, combining qualitatively and quantitatively generated data in their study of cross cultural relations, such as societal culture, organizational culture and organizational leadership. GLOBE provides an understanding of cultural variables that are significant when evaluating leadership and organizational processes. The result of the study identifies how cultural differences affect organizational leadership and the relationship to key account customers. GLOBE extends Hofstede's (1980) cultural dimensions, applying more variables and conceptualizing each dimension in two ways: *practices* or "as is", and *values* or "should be". Thus, values and practices of respondents from the participating organizations were compared. As a result, nine variables emerged, which will be used in the following paragraph. In Table 4.1, the nine different dimensions of House et al. (2004) are presented.

*Table 4.1: The 9 Cultural Dimensions in GLOBE*

| In-group Collectivism | Institutional Collectivism | Humane Orientation |
|---|---|---|
| Power Distance | Gender Egalitarianism | Future Orientation |
| Uncertainty Avoidance | Performance Orientation | Assertiveness |

Source: House et al. (2004, p. 993)

## Environmental Factors

In continuation of the above section, it is now time to consider which environmental factors affect Indian culture. But first, we need a clear definition for this environmental phenomenon. For this purpose, we lean on the well-known theorist Jobber who states:

> *"The macro- and micro-environments shape the character of the opportunities and threats facing a company and are largely uncontrollable."*
> (Jobber, 2007, p. 78)

Handling this phenomenon requires a simple model to map the most important environmental factors in order to avoid the worst pit falls and threats. To describe overall environmental factors in India, this section uses the PESTEL model as a theoretical foundation (Jobber, 2007, p. 78 and Lynch, 1997, p. 60-120). The PESTEL model has been chosen, because it is widely used and well-known among economists for describing the most important country factors. This model takes many different factors into consideration: political-, economic-, social-, technological-, legislative- and environmental issues. The PESTEL model can be used to analyze three different spheres: local, national and international. In relation to this study, the choice, naturally, is to focus on the national level of analysis.

Political, social and legislative factors will here be examined together in describing key issues of India's unique democratic, social and legislative factors. All three factors are interconnected and need therefore a joint examination. Furthermore, economic factors are concentrating on the current situation in India, including growth rates and the impact of the financial crisis. Treatment of technological factors is here limited to focus on communication issues in a broad perspective. By doing so, the unraveling of a much more complex situation is avoided. Finally, environmental factors of the PESTEL analysis are completely left out from this section, as they have little relevance for the relationship management subject.

At this point, the framework has presented cultural and environmental factors, but this will only give insight into external factors. In extension of this, it is of great importance to turn the view towards the inside the company as well. Internal specifics must be identified before looking into relational management theory. These internal factors will be examined in the section below.

## Consideration of Company Specific Variables

The study assumes that not two companies are alike. Therefore, it is a necessity to make the reader aware of this assumption, because some variables can be viewed from different perspectives. The individual reader should take these variables into consideration when making use of it in a specific situation. At this level of debate, de Wit and Meyer's (2004, p. 13) perspectives should be seen as a source of inspiration for the many possible strategic approaches that can be put into play at the three levels. The discussion will contain the following three perspectives:

- Business level:     Inside-out vs. Outside-In
- Corporate level:    Portfolio vs. Integrated
- Network level:      Discrete vs. Embedded

These perspectives are, as stated, build on the paradoxes of de Wit and Meyer (2004). They each represent a relevant problem to be solved at different levels of analysis. As mentioned earlier, the relationship between the company and their suppliers tends to be one of disparity in terms of the diverse Indian culture. Different perspectives on strategic considerations are normally viewed as a question of fitting a puzzle, solving a dilemma or counterbalancing a trade-off. However, these perspectives do not seem to clarify certain aspects of strategic tensions. By considering strategic tensions as paradoxes, it provides a context for considering cross-cultural aspects.

As paradoxes consist of two opposites that are non-compatible, even though both opposites are simultaneously true, an understanding of this tension is needed. Through understanding both sides of the paradox, one side has to be chosen, at the expense of the other. This way of thinking is consistent with the approach that has to be developed when considering cross-cultural dimensions as presented by House et al. (2004, p. 989-992). Different cultures are as such difficult to integrate logically into an internally consistent unit. Concurrent with this notion, another important notion is defining culture as a 'wicked' problem as opposed to a 'tame' problem.

'Wicked' problems such as culture have the tendency to be problems of organized complexity where an answer to a problem constitutes twice as many new problems. Relationship management in a cross-cultural perspective is, on behalf of the above, a difficult variable to measure in terms of formulation of the problem, solving the problem and testing the solution to the problem, because no such infinite solution exists to 'wicked' problems. Only interconnectedness, complicatedness, uncertainty, ambiguity and conflict truly outline what 'wicked' problems are about.

### Inside-Out vs. Outside-In

This perspective has its origin in the paradox of deciding the level of market adaption. Should one adapt to the market through one's supply- and value chain, or endeavor to affect the market through one's resources by finding new markets, if necessary.

### Portfolio vs. Integrated

This perspective originates in the paradox of whether one on the one hand should have decentralized cooperation with low coordination with the ability to adapt to specific conditions at the business level, or on the other hand, the synergistic approach, which seeks to utilize information, resources and the competitive position through a high degree of centralization and high coordination between strategic business units.

### Discrete vs. Embedded

This perspective originates in the paradox of whether the cooperation should take a competitive stand in terms of the specific environment by avoiding resource dependence and opportunism, or if the cooperation should take a cooperative stand in terms of the specific environment by outsourcing non-core activities and through convergence of interests.

By considering these perspectives on the three tensions described, one has to understand that the specific strategic considerations of each company will in many ways affect how processes will be carried out further in the company's supply chain. Because of these so-called 'company specifics', no choice of company strategy is right or wrong. The choice has to be seen as a result of the company's culture and the environment by which it is surrounded. Fundamentally, this is a question of perceiving one's surroundings deterministically or not.

## Relationship Management in Practice

The literature review has so far explained how to deal with Indian culture, the environment in which it unfolds and which company considerations to keep in mind. In this sense, the next step will be more specifically focused on how relationships management is carried out under those conditions. In order to comprehend the research question correctly without having to make an interpretation, it is important to state it clearly. So what is relationship management? Furthermore, what is meant by an Indian context? By relationship management is meant the methods that companies use to interact with customers and particularly key suppliers. When carrying out our business study in an Indian context, it is implied that an analysis of the environment in which Indian businesses operates is carried out.

## Key Account Supplier Management

Frow and Payne (2009) state some important elements that are worth considering when dealing with key suppliers. They define relationship management as:

> *"...the strategic management of relationships with all relevant stakeholders in order to achieve long term shareholder value. Critical tasks include identification of relevant relational forms for different stakeholders and the segments and subgroups within them and the optimal management of interactions within these stakeholder networks."* (Frow and Payne, 2009, p. 9)

But why is relationship management relevant when dealing with key suppliers? As implied, the 'key suppliers' are of the upmost importance when creating shareholder value. Therefore, it is necessary to deal with these suppliers in a substantially different way than with other suppliers. Keeping this in mind, we use the following definition of 'key account management':

> *"Key account management is a strategy used by suppliers to target and serve high-potential customers with complex needs by providing them with special treatment in the areas of marketing, administration and service."* (Jobber and Lancaster, 2009, p. 282)

However, this study reverses the supply chain and emphasizes the necessity of the company having a proactive approach towards key account suppliers, as they are of significant importance to the company's ability to obtain its goals. When dealing with a 'key account relationship', the buyer and seller are mutually willing to enter into a long-term partnership with greater risk-sharing. Risks are shared more, because the more the two organizations involved share information, build up common procedures and customize products with each other, the more the two organizations become dependent on each other. This means that if the two organizations stop their long-term partnership, a lot of time and work will be lost. At the same time, it will cost a lot of resources to obtain a similar position with other suppliers or customers. So how can relational strength in a partnership be measured? Millman and Wilson (1995) identify six steps of relational stages/status as portrayed in Figure 4.1. In order to understand this figure and the different levels of relations, a short explanation of the steps is briefly described in the following.

*Pre-KAM.* This stage involves identifying accounts with enough potential to avoid wasting investments on organizations, which will not contribute to the overall turnover or with essential resources for the overall activities.

*Early-KAM.* This is the early step, where the selling company seeks to convince the customer of the benefits from greater cooperation. In order to fully understand the value-adding process, the customer's decision-making unit needs to be understood, together with related problems and opportunities. After this, the selling company is able to treat the customer as a "key account".

*Figure 4.1: The Key Account Management Process*

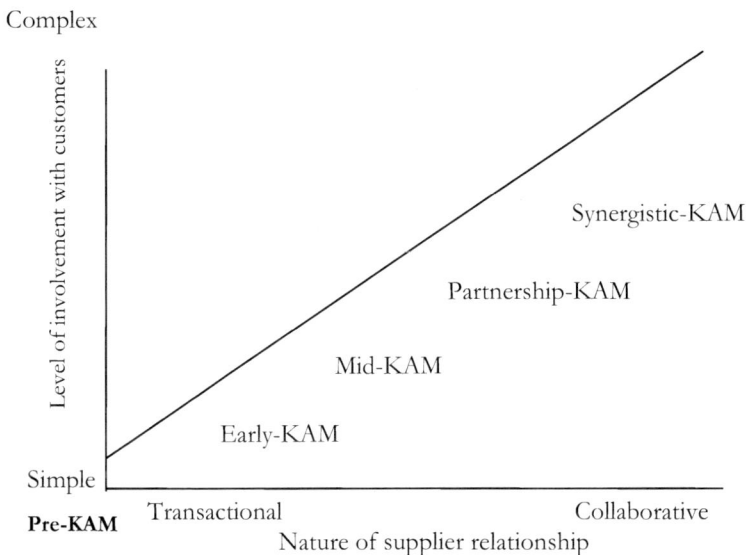

Source: Own compilation, based on Jobber and Lancaster (2009, p. 290)

*Mid-KAM.* Trust has now been established and cooperation will now tend to involve all parts of the organization, including senior management. The supplier is now one of a small number of preferred sources.

*Partnership-KAM.* The supplier has now become an important strategic resource. The level of trust will encourage sharing sensitive information and activities will move to joint problem-solving. The buying company is now challenging nearly all of its business in the relevant product group(s) to the one supplier, and there will be a written formalized partnership agreement between the two organizations over a time period of at least three years.

*Synergistic-KAM.* This is the highest stage of partnership that two organizations can achieve. Buyer and seller do not see each other as two separate organizations anymore, but as a part of a larger goal. Joint board meetings and joint board business planning as well as common research and development take place. Unnecessary costs between the firms are removed and common procedures are fully integrated.

*Uncoupling-KAM.* The cooperation is split up due to some kind of disagreement or breach of the agreement between the two organizations. The most common reason to a cooperation split is a change of key staff in charge of the relations for the two companies (Millman and Wilson, 1995).

Further investigation of the third research question considers an implementation approach.

## Implementation of Relational Strategies

Implementing a relational strategy in an organization can give some difficulties (Guenzi et al., 2007; Wengler et al., 2006). Wengler et al. (2006) found in their exploratory study some trends of implications in the implementation process of key account management in various companies. They found that the implementation process is characterized by numerous conflicts, communication difficulties and high complexity. Guenzi et al. (2007) found in their exploratory study of those companies three different relational behavior strategies: customer-oriented selling, adaptive selling and team selling. A short description of these three types of strategies will follow to be able to understand the context.

*Customer-Oriented Selling.* The company tries to adopt a win-win approach, where salespeople become customer partners. Willingness to reject short-term profits over long-term cooperation needs to be in focus.

*Adaptive Selling.* There is here a high level of long-term thinking. The selling company seeks a great amount of information regarding its key accounts, in order to be able to customize products according to their needs. The idea behind adaptive selling is to increase the buying company's dependence on the selling company.

*Team Selling.* The sales process can in many cases be complex and require answers in many different aspects. Therefore, the sales process can require a team of persons from the companies who have responsibility from different areas. These areas can be prices, production and technical aspects in order to get more quality out of the meetings.

## The Overall Framework for Analysis

Inspired by de Wit and Meyer (2004), this study will build on a framework containing the following three steps: Context, content and process. These three stages are to be seen as an iterative process in which they all affect each other.

The first stage, 'context', is linked to research question 1 and 2 and contains the 9 dimensions from House et al. (2004) and the PESTEL environment analysis. The second stage, 'content', is linked to research question 3 and covers the business specific variables that are adopted into the analysis framework. The third stage, 'process', is linked to research question 4 and examines Wengler et al.'s (2006) 'three relational behavior strategies' and Millman and Wilson's (1995) 'key account management process'. Figure 4.2 is showing the study's workflow. The figure provides the framework on which the following empirical analysis is based.

In Figure 4.2, de Wit and Meyer's (2004) overall framework, 'Process, Content and Context', is adopted to clarify the different levels of analysis that have to be considered when working with Relationship Management. The 'Context', in which the 'Content' and 'Process' is shaped, has its theoretical stand in House et al. (2004) and the 9 cultural dimensions from the GLOBE study. Together with the 6 factors of PESTEL (Jobber, 2007), both cultural and environmental variables constitute the 'Context'. Contrary to both 'Context' and 'Process', 'Content' has not been given a set of variables by which the level of analysis can be explained. The reason why this has been done is rooted in the very different ontological and epistemological stances by which every company can be viewed. Instead, a discussion on how companies dissociate from each other is grounded in the three perspectives of de Wit and Meyer (2004).

*Figure 4.2: Factors to consider when managing relationships*

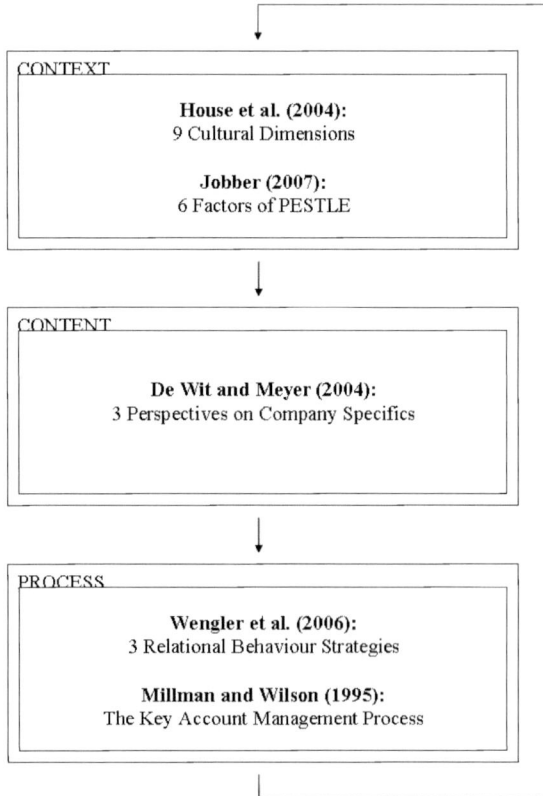

```
┌────────────────────────────────────────────────┐
│                                                  │
│   CONTEXT                                        │
│   ┌──────────────────────────────────────────┐  │
│   │            House et al. (2004):           │  │
│   │            9 Cultural Dimensions          │  │
│   │                                           │  │
│   │              Jobber (2007):               │  │
│   │              6 Factors of PESTLE          │  │
│   └──────────────────────────────────────────┘  │
│                                                  │
│   CONTENT                                        │
│   ┌──────────────────────────────────────────┐  │
│   │          De Wit and Meyer (2004):         │  │
│   │      3 Perspectives on Company Specifics   │  │
│   └──────────────────────────────────────────┘  │
│                                                  │
│   PROCESS                                        │
│   ┌──────────────────────────────────────────┐  │
│   │           Wengler et al. (2006):           │  │
│   │        3 Relational Behaviour Strategies   │  │
│   │                                           │  │
│   │          Millman and Wilson (1995):        │  │
│   │       The Key Account Management Process   │  │
│   └──────────────────────────────────────────┘  │
│                                                  │
└────────────────────────────────────────────────┘
```

Source: Own compilation, based on House et al. (2004),
Jobber (2007), de Wit and Meyer (2004), Wengler et al. (2006),
Millman and Wilson (1995)

These three perspectives should be kept in mind when managing relationships in practice. Whatever the result of the interactions in 'Content' might be, it affects the way the 'Process' is initiated. In 'Process', the relational behavior strategies by Wengler et al. (2006) and the Key Account Management Process by Millman and Wilson (1995) have shaped the theoretical stand. The idea is that culture and environment, along with the three perspectives, will affect which type of Relational Behavior Strategy is chosen. Further, this choice will affect where in the Key Account Management Process one will enter and by which speed one will move through the process. When choosing the overall framework of de Wit and

Meyer (2004), it should be noted that this 'step by step' model is only constructed for pedagogical reasons. It provides a fair chance to understand the mechanisms in the Relationship Management Process. However, de Wit and Meyer's (2004) framework should be looked upon as a framework where every variable is interdependent with other variables.

## Analysis

### Cultural Differences

This section describes which cultural issues affect the way of doing business in India. In accordance with the analysis framework, this refers to the step 'context'. As pointed out in the literature review, the GLOBE project by House et al. (2004) provides nine cultural dimensions, which will be analyzed according to the observations from the field study. The contribution by GLOBE is a helpful tool to understand Indian culture and the dimension to be aware of. The nine dimensions that influence companies' decisions about doing business in India are: *In-group Collectivism, Institutional Collectivism, Humane Orientation, Power Distance, Gender Egalitarianism, Future Orientation, Uncertainty Avoidance, Performance Orientation and Assertiveness.*

As mentioned previously, India is a mix of many different cultures, religions, races and languages. India is one of the oldest civilizations on Earth, with a cultural historical background dating back more than 5000 years. It is the largest democracy in the world, but hardly the most effective and efficient. By 2025, India will be the world's 5th largest consumer market with potential growth rates above 5 percent the next 20-35 years (McKinsey, 2007). Having constant growth and a highly qualified workforce makes India attractive to operate in, as well as cooperate with.

According to observations during the field study, it is possible to create and apply a general image of the country, despite the many differences. India's diverse economy is comprised of conventional village farming as well as modern agriculture, a wide range of modern industries and a large number of services and handicrafts. Important points to understand are main elements in Indian culture, such as the way Indians communicate, as well as understanding Indian traditions and the caste system. Business professionals in India have a basic rule: they don't like to say no, highly differentiating them from Westerners. This makes the choice of words crucial, when aiming at a specific output. More so, it is important as a Danish manager to be at the same level as the people you're going into business with. This will be examined later in this chapter. These are

105

important aspects to take into consideration, when nurturing relations and building a business. Another variable which was retrieved from the studies was the direct way of interacting with one another. Indians ask personal questions right away. If one is not willing to invest in a personal relation, which can include questions about one's on family life, no business deals will be closed. Likewise, business contracts are not taken into consideration unless a personal relation has been developed first.

## Dimensions to Deal with in Relation to Indian Suppliers

According to the nine dimensions of House et al. (2004), India is very much a pluralistic culture. Even so, there is a tendency for India to score high on variables such as 'collectivism', 'humane orientation' and 'power distance'. Focusing on 'collectivism', it can be seen that the family unit is very important in Indian society (House et al., 2004, p. 991). Indian people perceive themselves as part of a collective dimension (House et al., 2004, p. 11). They constantly see themselves as part of an organization or family. It is expected that people show loyalty and support toward their group/organization in return for protection and a sense of belonging. However, for employees a high degree of loyalty is not expected. At this level, there is a high degree of replacement – not because employees are fired, but because the employees are switching jobs.

In all of the visited companies, 'human resource management' / 'humane orientation' was a familiar issue. Not every company seemed to find it necessary to implement it though, at least not according to Western standards. Accidents at work are required to be reported to the leader (House et al., 2004, p. 990). There are many laws to protect people from begging, torture by the police etc. It's not implemented very well though. If a personal tragedy occurs, Indians offer to provide help. This behavior will improve their next life according to their religion.

The caste system is a major influence on the high 'power distance' in India. Another contributor to this is nearly 200 years under British rule (House et al., 2004, p. 991). The formal structure of the society has a huge impact on Indian organizations. Businesses are hierarchical and work titles are being used to show status in the organization. According to the field study, everyone has different privileges depending on status, which in practice are clearly understood.

'Gender egalitarianism' has a low score in India, but is rising. So, it is a male dominated culture, though more and more women are accessing jobs at the higher levels of the hierarchy. This low gender egalitarianism was recognized by the companies and did not have any influence when interacting in a business relation with women.

There is great focus on future development; thus 'future orientation' scores high. The government provides tax breaks on savings to help 'future orientation' (House et al., 2004, p. 990). Indians have great interest in developing how to conduct business and retain knowledge from the West. This is something which Western companies can benefit from. Not only does India have great knowledge and eagerness to build relations, it also has cheap labor and production. India defies the financial crisis the rest of the world is suffering from. Economic growth is rising alongside with the Indian middleclass. As a Western company, there is great potential to discover sectors of growth in India (Frijs-Madsen, 2009, p. 26-41).

In continuation of this, India has low 'uncertainty avoidance'. This makes Indians open to their environment and new initiatives. This has made it easy to implement western business routines. As mention earlier, every business begins with a strong relationship. Business contracts come second, as contracts do not have the same status as in the west. In India, business relationships are built on close and strong ties between business partners (House et al., 2004, p. 13). As a result of this, contracts made with Indian companies are typically significantly shorter than both European and American contracts. There is high need for contracts when foreign companies do business in India, but the relationship between business partners must be taken into consideration first.

With respect to 'performance orientation', the first step is to understand the dimensions of Equal vs. Unequal. In India, teachers are respected in schools, parents at home and bosses in offices. Indians therefore accept the unequal dimension. The caste system in India is a good example of the acceptance of inequality in status and privileges. As a consequence of the system, Indians do not think for themselves as much as Danes do. With this in mind, employees do what is being said and no more. Even so, India has a moderate score of 'performance orientation'.

'Assertiveness' is more difficult to comment on and perhaps a low to moderate score is most reasonable. What is considered appropriately assertive can vary by culture. House et al. (2004) defines 'assertiveness' as the degree to which individuals in organizations or societies are assertive, confrontational, and aggressive in social relationships. Because of the social and economic structuring of society, Indians do not express themselves as openly and honestly as we do in the west. Religion also makes Indians accept their fate more than westerners.

To summarize, Indians have strong family ties, they feel affection for education and are willing to do hard work. It can be said that India's strength lies in low cost production and that Indians face difficult and new situations with a smile and harder work. The ability to communicate effectively, exercise control and provide direction is an important requirement when doing business in India. Hence, the following success criteria arise, as listed in Table 4.2. This table is an excellent starting ground for Western companies, when considering entering the Indian market. It gives preconceptions about Indians, which can be beneficial for a first meeting.

*Table 4.2: Five Things To Be Aware Of When Doing Business in India*

Foreigners doing business in India may experience great cultural differences that can result in major delays in projects etc. These cultural differences can vary from small differences to more substantial differences. In order to accommodate these differences, an approach could be to reverse communication. Instead of telling what we expect the status should be on a given project, one should let the Indians present the status of a project and how far they have come. In this way, views are formed and presented, which one can act on. This solution would create better teamwork and relationships between the western and Indian companies.

**A Yes Can Mean No**

Indian people do not like to refuse each other, tasks or projects, and as a result of this they avoid saying "no". Generally, they think it is insulting to say no, and in the lower social levels they will always say yes even when they are aware that they cannot fulfill their promise. If an Indian says: "I will see what I can do" is it actually his or her way of saying "no" without insulting anyone. This only applies for the lower social levels, in the higher end of society the formality for declining and accepting is similar to those in the West. Here, yes means yes and no means no.

**Indians Shake Their Heads the Other Way When Nodding**

The Indian people are generally forthcoming and friendly. They nod when they communicate in order to be friendly. However, foreigners should be aware of the fact that Indians shake their heads the other way when nodding.

**Be Patient**

Personal relationships are very important for successful business relationships in India. It is important to be patient and create a social atmosphere. You cannot expect to do business in India at the first meeting.

**Indians Expect Hierarchy**

There is a hierarchy in both age and gender. It is important to show respect for elders and even though women are increasingly entering the business world, it is still preferred to do business with men.  One should bring a business card with a title along for meetings, because it helps in the hierarchy. If you do not have a title on your business card, it can be an advantage to make an extra set for use in India.

**Time Perception**

Time perception in India is very different from time perception in both Europe and the USA. In India, time is plentiful and there is always tomorrow. As a result of this, punctuality is not an issue as it is in Western countries. In India, it is not an insult to be late, and meetings often start later than scheduled. The country's infrastructure is partly the cause for this as it can take from 45 minutes to several hours to drive 15 km.

## The Relationship Between India and the West From a Cultural Perspective

The description of Indian culture and the many different dimensions between India and the West set the ground rules for doing business. The study showed that cooperation between two countries contains parts of each country's culture. Despite the fact that westerners and easterners see the world differently, they do business together with success by exploiting each other's advantages. A compromise was found, which both parties found satisfactory. In light of the analyzed cultural part, business relationships between Indian and Western companies can be illustrated as below.

*Figure 4.3: The Cooperative Relationships Model*

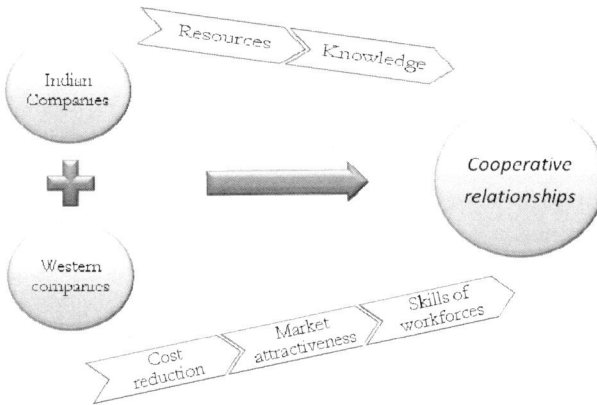

Source: Own compilation

Figure 4.3 presents the cooperative relationships between Indian and Western companies. The model illustrates what the motivation is to enter into a relationship with each other. The motives that emerged from the study were very different, rooted in each country's culture. The model shows that there are great benefits for each country in collaborating.

## Benefits for Indian Companies

The study of the companies showed a great interest in taking knowledge from Western companies. This is to optimize business processes, work more efficiently and thus become more attractive. In order to compete globally, Indian companies need to incorporate some Western standards. An example of this is quality, as required by Western consumers.

Resources are another thing that the Indian companies found interesting. Indian employees can learn much from Western technology and knowledge about (the effective and efficient use of) the technology. Western companies are investing, e.g. buildings and roads, which are badly needed in India.

## Benefits for Western Companies

Cost reduction is a very important factor for Western companies to enter the Indian market. The cheap labor makes the Indian market very attractive, rather than the domestic. Another motive is cheap products. Compared to the example of China, Indian products are regarded to be of higher quality. As mentioned earlier, India has a very large, high-skilled workforce. This makes it profitable to make use of either outsourcing or off-shoring (discussed in a separate chapter). This must be seen in light of India's size, which is a big advantage. The study showed that the purchasing power is huge. This should be seen beyond India's high growth and population, as previously described. There is great potential for growth and economic benefits, which can make Western companies even stronger on national and international markets.

It can be concluded that the motives for entering collaboration between Indian and Western companies are different, but this means that both parties get a lot out of the relationship and are highly motivated. The main motive for Western companies to choose India as the relationship partner is cost reduction, market attractiveness and skills of workforces. During the study of culture, it became clear that the next step is to analyze the environmental factors before focusing on key account management.

## Environmental Factors

This section describes which environmental issues affect the way of doing business in India. In accordance with the analysis framework this also refers to the step: 'context'.

During the field study trip, we discovered how different market conditions are, compared to a western marketplace. Therefore, it is important to look at environmental factors influencing Indian culture. There are a lot of different areas to pay attention to, but the focus will be on what is relevant for India: how the global recession is affecting business in India, the huge democracy, the Indian way of communicating, and finally the decision whether to do business on the domestic market or focusing on export.

## India and the Global Recession

The Indian economy is strong and is working its steady way through the global recession due to continuous overall growth, which however has fallen slightly from 9 percent in 2008 to around 5.6 percent in 2009 (Frijs-Madsen, 2009, p. 2-29). This growth level is still among the world's highest, despite the downturn during the financial crisis. An explanation for this can be found in the increasing population growth in India's middleclass, which boosts the economy. Nevertheless, this growth in middleclass does hide some of the impacts that the recession has caused. To mention a few, downturns in the real estate market and increases in the pricing range of food are having a huge impact on especially the agriculture sector in India, which numbers 700 million people. However, the government is naturally trying to protect this important sector by offering additional support in form of financial help packages. In general, India is managing the crisis quite well compared to western countries, due to the low level of export. Therefore, continuous growth on the domestic market keeps the overall growth rate at a decent 5.6 percent. But there are exceptions. The software industry in India, for example, is closely linked with and dependent on western countries. It has thus suffered from the crisis and is expecting a huge fall in growth rate, from approximately 30 percent to 16 percent. It is worth to mention that most of the growth is driven by the large amount of money invested from western countries.

## Democracy

India has one of the world's largest populations, which is a great difference compared to western countries like Denmark. This phenomenon makes competition conditions very different from what we know in smaller Western countries. In India, manpower is the smallest problem, it doesn't matter whether you need a hundred or a thousand employees, because there is always a big base to recruit from. An example of this is that the production-unit at one of the firms visited could be expanded with 200 employees within a couple of weeks. This is of course a great competitive factor promoting India. But there are also some costs to having such a large population. Some other big societies comparable to India are run by dictators, which does not harmonize with our way of thinking. India is the world's biggest democracy, which fits with our mental conviction, but in such a big country, it means that a lot of decisions take a very long time, because everyone has to be heard. The leaders of the companies we interviewed all joked that in many matters a dictatorship would be easier for Indian development all together. They for example pinpointed the bad infrastructure as an area to improve, but because of democracy, it takes a long time. In China, they are able to make a new road the day after the decision, but in India every landowner has to be heard. Democracy is also affecting the rules and laws. It is our opinion, that India has a lot of rules concerning almost as many areas as in Denmark. An example of this is the non-liberal policy towards the labor market. In India, an employee cannot be dismissed after a 6 months employment period. Some of those we spoke to admitted that it is common to dismiss employees before the 6 months are over and reinstate them afterwards to get around the rule, but actually it is not accepted if the conflict comes to court. Laws are being transformed to western standards. For example, it is now legal for a foreign company to own 100 percent of an Indian company, which is making the process of doing business in India a lot easier for foreign companies.

## Communication

Communication is very important to Indians. Communication should not only be by email, telephone etc. This kind of communication is considered impersonal. Besides this, the caste system plays a significant role in communicating. People communicating have to be at the same level of caste or business hierarchy. Only when the personal relation has been build between customer and supplier, it is possible to talk business and hereby make transactions. This will be considered more carefully later in this chapter.

## Domestic Market or Export?

The companies visited by the relationship management group were at this time only serving the domestic market. This is however not surprising, as many foreign companies have discovered the huge potential and growth rate of the Indian market- Even in a period with financial crisis there is stable growth. They see this market as a very stable market with a growth rate higher than almost any other country. This makes it very lucrative for almost all companies to engage in the Indian market.

At this point, cultural and environmental factors have been examined, but this has only provided insight into external factors. In extension of this, it is of great importance to turn the view inside the company as well. Internal specifics must be indentified and taken into account before looking at relational management in practice.

## Consideration of Company Specific Variables

This section describes which company specific issues can impact the way relational key account management is carried out. In accordance with the analysis framework, this also refers to the step 'content'.

### Inside-Out vs. Outside-In

The relatively small number of companies visited during the fieldtrip all gave the impression of acting after the Outside-In perspective, adapting to the environment and not trying to shape it themselves. This is somehow not logical, as the Inside-Out perspective requires unique internal resources and is associated with large risk taking, which Indian society, according to research question 1, should be willing and able to. Furthermore, the workforce is well educated, which could be turned into a unique resource. So there is great potential to Western companies to aim for the Inside-Out perspective, but yet again, it is up to the company to decide according to one's risk aversion, the overall strategy and the organizational culture.

### Portfolio vs. Integrated

The companies visited in India gave the impression of acting from a portfolio perspective, rather than an integrated point of view. As such, the companies visited focused on their specific environment by having a decentralized organization with a low sense of coordination. This made it possible to adapt faster to the specific conditions at the business level. Therefore, it might be recommendable to choose an approximate portfolio strategy as Indian culture favors close relationships.

### Discrete vs. Embedded

The research conducted in India gave no indication of whether the companies chose the discrete perspective or the embedded perspective as a starting point. However, Indian companies favor strong relations to other companies. This makes the embedded perspective a possible approach between cross-cultural cooperation through convergence of interest. If Western companies favor adaption to the market at the business/corporate level, the discrete perspective might be the one of interest. The discrete perspective reduces resource dependence and the risk of opportunism between the two cooperating companies.

It is still up to the company though to decide how they act and how they will adapt to the specific surrounding environment, including the culture that is of great importance in a foreign country.

## Relationship Management in Practice

This section describes how key account supplier management should be carried out according to research question 1 and 2, which constituted the context. The company specific considerations mentioned in research question 3 will not be dealt with in this paragraph, but should be taken into mind when implemented by the reader to a real life specific situation. In accordance with the analysis framework, this paragraph refers to the step 'process'.

### Why Focus on Key Suppliers?

Working with management-related cross-cultural issues is not easy. Many aspects must be assessed and analyzed. As mentioned in the literature review, the focus of this chapter is on key account suppliers. According to Gruen (1997), companies spend on average six times more to acquire customers than they do to retain current customers (Gruen, 1997). The assumption is that the same issue will be valid for a company, if they are to find new suppliers instead of developing current relationships. Because developing new supplier relationships tend to be expensive, both due to identifying, negotiating contracts and developing routines, and particularly companies with special needs that demand collaborative solutions, key account supplier management is profitable. Therefore, there is an increasing tendency to have greater focus on current suppliers. This means more attention to the relationship with existing suppliers. Indian culture, as previously mentioned, is very direct and personal. The study showed that Indians were not very loyal to their partners if the relationship was not nurtured. Personal involvement in the relationship is important when building businesses together. This makes the key suppliers of particular importance. Western companies who want to have collaboration in India should have a strategy for key account suppliers to succeed.

### Implementation of Relational Behavior Strategies

Before choosing at which level of KAM cooperation the company seeks to commence, it is of importance to clarify which relational behavior is of interest for both parties in the corporation.

None of the companies visited expressed considerable difficulties in their implementation process. The research in India found that because Indian culture emphasizes strong relations between people, they quickly adapt behavioral strategies towards relationship building. Indian companies always seek to build a relationship with the other part. The strength of the relationship can of course vary, but it seems to be a fact, that the persons involved always seek a relation of higher or lower intensity. The research found that the companies visited were already working with these strategies. One of the companies interviewed clearly stated, that they would at any time choose to reject short-term profits in order to help one of their key accounts. This was the kind of long-term thinking the companies expressed. Another company had implemented the slogan "fewer clients, more attention" through the entire organization. The meaning of this was to seek close partnerships instead of having a big supplier portfolio.

As stated earlier, Indian culture emphasizes relations before transactions. It is normal in India to have five or more meetings before the first purchase. In this way, companies automatically gather information from the other part and find out what critical issues to focus on and which specific needs they have. Adaptive selling was also found highly relevant, because the companies expressed that they had a high demand for customized products. One of the most common relational strategies used in India is 'team selling'. When the volume of transactions and the relation between two organizations grow, a specific demand for team selling on the Indian market arises. As shown in Figure 4.4 beneath, all administrative levels between two interacting companies have to communicate/socialize in order to work out a successful relation.

*Figure 4.4: Interaction Between Companies When Building a Relationship*

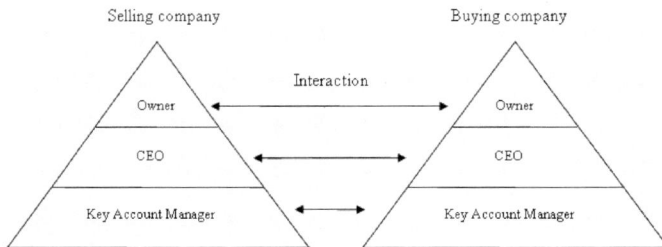

Source: Own compilation

## Key Account Management

As presented in the literature review, the key account management process is not easy. As illustrated and explained in Figure 4.2, both House et al.'s cultural dimensions, the output from the PESTEL analysis and de Wit and Meyer's strategic 'content' must be taken into consideration when managing key account relations management, especially when dealing with two cultures that are foreign to each other. Bear in mind that where the theory has its shortcomings, it can profitably be complemented with empirical findings, discussions and reflections and hereby lay down useful guidelines for the reader.

During the fieldtrip, it became quite clear that one of the essential conclusions made from investigating the visited companies was the fact that relations create transactions in India. You have to build up a relation before the first transaction between two organizations will take place; this was emphasized over and over by the visited companies. This is different from the way most Western companies work, i.e. the relationship is normally developed after the first transactions are made. That is why Indian companies in most cases start up in early-KAM and quickly move to mid-KAM, where Western companies start up in the pre-KAM stage. When trust has been established between the two organizations and the volume of transactions grows, they often move into partnership-KAM. A contact person at one of the companies visited, stated the following:

*"It applies for the whole world, that there would not be any need for sales guys if you did not need relations. But there is a stronger need for relations in India than in western countries".*

Another interviewed person stated:

*"If a foreign company and an Indian company start a cooperation of more or less intensity, it will definitely be the Indian company who will start moving into a closer relation with the other part".*

These statements are a common belief throughout the Indian companies interviewed. From this, it can be stated that Western companies have to adapt this strong relational approach, in order to be successful when dealing with Indian companies. The meetings with Indian companies also showed that all the companies visited were too small, compared to their key-suppliers, to engage in synergistic-KAM. If the purchased volume is only a small part of the buying company's overall sourcing volume, the buying company will not have any interest in moving to synergistic-KAM. However, the opposite situation can also occur. Although the supplying company is small, its product or service might be of great importance to the buying company. Here, synergistic-KAM is a possibility.

To summarize the research findings, relationship management is highly present on the Indian market. Indian culture and the way they interact with each other emphasize strong relations, even before a transaction has occurred. Therefore, foreign companies need to have Wengler et al.'s (2006) three relational behavior strategies in mind. Without these relational approaches, it will be difficult for a Western company to be successful in India and initiate a high level KAM-corporation. This is expected by Indian culture.

## Conclusion

During the field study, it was discovered how relationship management is being used in an Indian context. It was found that most relations were quite strong and very personal, which make key account management exceedingly important.

### Culture

Many cultural issues impact the way of doing business in India. The main motives are personal relations with whom you are doing business with. This led to investigate cultural variables which are significant when evaluating organizational processes and the relationship to key account suppliers. The GLOBE research program was used to investigate which implications culture brings. In order to handle the implications, Table 4.2 shows five things to be particularly aware of when doing business in India. The caste system affects the way of communicating. It is important that you are at the same level. Indians have different privileges depending on status. In India, there is massive focus on 'future orientation', which Western companies can benefit from. Indians are open to conduct business and retain knowledge from the West. The companies are hierarchical and because of this Indians do not express themselves as openly and honestly as we do in the West. The ability to exercise control and provide direction is one of the most important requirements when doing business in India.

### Environment

Environmental factors that influence doing business in India can be summarized as follows: In India, there is currently a huge growth in the middle class, which makes it very lucrative to stake on the local market, as the demand for western goods is exploding and it seems to be a continuous development. Regarding communication, it is important to notice that the

117

caste system in India is of great importance and it is only possible to communicate with a person on the same level as yourself.

Furthermore, one has to bear in mind that India is the world largest democracy, and everyone is allowed an opinion on everything. This can make the decision making process slow and difficult. Therefore, plenty of time and manpower is needed when doing business in India. Finally, India has labor laws protecting individuals' rights, including minimum wage laws and guarantees that a laborer cannot be dismissed after 6 months without a retirement benefit plan.

## Company Specific Variables

The empirical findings related to de Wit and Meyer's (2004) three perspectives are not to be seen as a strict guideline, but as a source of inspiration for the reader. Nevertheless, examination during the fieldtrip indicates that companies in India tend to have a preference for using the 'outside-in perspective', where the environment shapes the organization and not the other way around, as the 'inside-out perspective' states. There will however, for the daring company, be a possibility to exploit the well educated workforce and the low uncertainty avoidance in Indian culture to try out the inside-out perspective.

Regarding the 'portfolio versus integrated' perspective, there was made a slight recommendation of the portfolio perspective, as this will gain a faster response time to market and in general handle closer relationships better. In addition to close relationships, we concluded in research question 1, that the Indian culture truly favors this. Should a company though be in special need of a highly integrated organization, they may not be frightened by this recommendation. They should just take into consideration to maintain a fast response rate to the market and to nurture their relationships. Finally, concerning the 'discrete and embedded perspective', Indian companies favor strong relations to other companies. This makes the embedded perspective a promising approach in cross-cultural cooperation through convergence of interest. From some Western companies' point of view, they might however favor the discrete perspective, as it reduces the independence to external resources. This raises a slight conflict of interest that has to be individually balanced, so both the Indian and the Western party are satisfied with the corporation.

## Relationship Management

Indian culture favors building a strong relationship as a basis for further interactions with new customers. That is why Indians, in most cases, start up in the early-KAM and move fast into mid-KAM. When trust has been established, they often move into partnership-KAM. Because Indian companies always seek to build a relationship with the other part, they quickly adapt behavioral strategies towards relationship building. The most common relational strategy used in India is "team selling". When the volume of transactions and the relation between two organizations grows, a specific demand for team selling on the Indian market arises.

As a natural consequence of the above mentioned, strategic considerations should be used as a mindset for understanding not only the cultural factors, environmental factors, organizational factors and factors regarding relationship management, but for understanding the broader implications, which is a part of every cross-cultural relationship. As such, it is important to understand that these strategic mindsets affect the cultural factors and hereby the environmental factors and the factors affecting relationship management, including key account management.

# CHAPTER 5

# Corporate Social Responsibility

*Merete Søberg Christensen, Jette Lindvig Hansen, Christine Madsen, Martin Raun Madsen, Henrik Storck*

## Abstract

*Cultural differences between India and Denmark are large, which also includes the way CSR is viewed. Therefore, it is important for Danish companies to understand how appropriate CSR management is considered in India. Among others, India has a long tradition for various philanthropic initiatives. This chapter gives insight into how CSR is considered in India. Through empirical data collected in Danish subsidiaries in India, examples are given on how CSR is viewed and what activities these companies are engaged in. Lastly, the chapter gives CSR recommendations for management to consider when doing business in India.*

## Introduction

This section will introduce the global context of Corporate Social Responsibility (CSR), whereupon a short introduction to Indian society regarding CSR will follow. Subsequently, the chapter's structure will be outlined and explained.

To understand what CSR is about, it is important to understand the background of CSR, including its drivers. One of the main drivers is globalization, especially the negative aspects and the new challenges that globalization of the economy has brought for business all over the world (van Liempd 2007, p. 6). Globalization has contributed to an increasing number of businesses that choose to outsource or off-shore (parts of) their production and, in line with that, the marketplace has gone from a national to a global scale. Outsourcing and off-shoring of operations, sales and administrative processes to low wage countries, such as India and China, results in financial benefits, but also creates new challenges with respect to ethics and social responsibility. As production, sales and administrative units are outsourced, so are the ethical and social responsibilities. The end producer usually does not fully control sub-suppliers, even though the end producer is still in danger to be held responsible by stakeholders for breaches of human rights, use of child labor, environmental spills, poisonous production processes or other unethical environmental and social activities (ibid., p. 7).

Information and communication processes have also undergone a huge development. The amount, speed and spread of information have grown exponentially, which means that business' transparency and visibility have increased as well. This development has made it much more difficult for individual businesses to hide the effects of unethical behavior and even to behave unethically (ibid, p. 6). The focus, in the media and among stakeholders, on scandals and the fact that many companies tried to hide unethical behavior, has contributed to the increased global interest in CSR. Hence, apparent indicators of the need for attention towards this specific topic are the many scandals, which have dominated the CSR field within recent years (www.corpwatch.org). An example is Wal-Mart and the highly published incidence of the polluted baby milk, or Nike and the controversial working conditions for Chinese production employees (ibid.). To avoid more scandals in the future, it is important that businesses consider strategic aspects and adopt a proactive approach towards problems concerning CSR.

## India

Within recent years, India has developed from being categorized as a developing country to a newly industrialized country – classified as medium developed cf. UN Human Development Reports (2009). The sudden shift in categorization has resulted in India today being stereotyped as a country with a rich culture, maharajas, and spirituality on the one hand and immense poverty in extensive slum districts on the other hand. The stereotype is partly true, but modern India is rapidly detaching itself from this interpretation (Adolphsen 2004, p. 15). Modern India has many Western character traits, especially American, which for example can be seen in Indian marketing and local brands in shopping malls.

Behind the modern surface, Indians still retain their profound traditions solidly. Among those is the strict hierarchy of society, based on membership of castes and social rank, which is a cause for the difference in affluence that exists in Indian society. In this connection, it is essential to realize that India in many ways still is at a completely different developmental stage than the Western world – most European countries and the US are classified as very high developed cf. UN Human

Development Reports (2009). This implies different demands and terms for doing business. Regarding the CSR perspective, this is a central focal point. The discussion of India's development stage of society will be elaborated on in some of the following paradox discussions in this chapter. As will be argued, a country's development phase does have a great impact on the views on and choices of CSR approach cf. the paradoxes in this chapter's empirical section.

Striving towards the modern world exists simultaneously with strong traditions in India. This implies that the new prosperity in India often has not caused a change in traditional mentality as in dissociating from or moving away from traditional spiritualism. In India, where the elite view themselves at the forefront of technological development, respect for both traditions and for advanced technology causes no problems (Adolphsen 2004, p. 14). This must be seen in light of the fact that the general Indian population has no moral problems with social injustice. Social injustice is an unknown concept in India (ibid.). In a CSR perspective, this view of social injustice must lead to challenges and implications, when doing business in India.

The rest of this chapter consist of, first, a methodology section, followed by a short theory section, leading to the main part with a focus on the empirical data. The chapter is completed with a conclusion including managerial recommendations for doing business in India from a CSR perspective.

## Methodology

This section covers the methodology used for the research and presents the main research question. Subsequently, the limitations of the study are discussed and the results are evaluated.

The main reason to write this chapter is to get an idea of how CSR is applied in India and what to consider regarding CSR, when doing business in India. Thus, the main research question of this chapter is:

**Research Question:** *How is CSR considered in India?*

Understanding the theoretical basis of CSR before going to India was crucial. The study began with a literature review to get a general understanding of CSR. This is reflected in the theory section of this chapter. However, this chapter will attach the greatest importance to empiricism.

Partly through reading scientific articles and brainstorms, partly due to the current increased focus on sustainability as an aspect of CSR in Denmark, the chapter's initial focal area became the environment. With the focal area situated, the research questions to the empirical part of the research were constructed. First, a set of general questions were outlined regarding the understanding of CSR and CSR-policies in the companies. After these opening questions, the questions became more specific, primarily concerning cultural differences and environmental aspects.

The empirical research included a total of 5 visits to Danish subsidiaries in Chennai and Bangalore and a lecture from the Danish Trade Council in Bangalore. Beginning with general questions, the hope was that the respondents would be more willing to answer more sensitive questions afterwards. It was the intention that the interviews with the Danish subsidiaries in India would be semi-structured, where the subsidiaries would receive the questions in advance. The respondents would then have the possibility of being prepared before the visits, and our job would be to listen and ask clarifying questions.

However, from the first visit on, it became quite clear that the questions showed to be insufficient, because the CSR focus in India was not on the environment. When asked about CSR, respondents typically answered on social and philanthropic aspects of CSR, and not so much environmental aspects. On that background, the focus in the field shifted away from primarily environmental questions to more general CSR questions, depending on the main focus of the company.

Even though the respondents did not focus on the environmental aspects of the research questions, the gathered empirical data did provide useful data for the analysis regarding CSR in general, especially regarding the social aspects. In this connection, it is also important to emphasize that the lack of focus on environmental aspects regarding CSR in itself is a usable result. The rest of the analysis deals with core issues about CSR, when doing business in India.

Unfortunately, the analysis will have some limitations, as always. As mentioned, all of the visited companies were Danish subsidiaries. This means that their CSR-policy might be different from independent Indian companies' CSR policies. Danish and Indian companies do have different approaches to CSR. Another limitation could be the locations of the subsidiaries. All the subsidiaries are located in the southern part of India. The situation regarding CSR could look different in Northern India – given that India is a large diverse country, consisting of many regions with different laws, languages and subcultures.

The empirical study will still be relevant though, as it will be analyzed in relation to the following theory section. In the empirical section, the collected data will be analyzed and recommendations about what to consider about CSR in India will be given in the conclusion.

## Theoretical CSR Definition

This section contains the chapter's theory section. Firstly, the definition of CSR is set out. In relation to the definitions, it is important to emphasize that the purpose of this chapter is not to examine and discuss the notion or development of CSR, but rather to adopt a general accepted understanding. Subsequently, a framework for guidelines regarding CSR is introduced. It should be mentioned that the completed literature review will not be summarized in this section, but will be articulated in the empirical section instead.

Numerous different definitions of the notion CSR exist. In this chapter, the discussion of these notions will take their basis in the following definitions:

> "*Corporate Social Responsibility is a concept whereby companies integrate social and environmental concerns in their business operations and in their interaction with their stakeholders on a voluntary basis.*" EU white paper (2001)

and

> "*The social responsibility of business encompasses the economic, legal, ethical, and discretionary expectations that society has of organizations at a given point of time.*" Carroll (1979)

These definitions encompass central aspects of the basic understanding of CSR. Especially, it should be noted that Carroll (1979) expresses CSR as societal expectations at a given point of time. This can be interpreted to mean that the development stage of society is a key factor with regards to the definition of CSR, which further can be transferred to the question, whether the Western understanding of CSR is at all practicable in the East.

The definitions do not explicitly focus on the different motives for doing CSR. This is why Figure 5.1 is included, which shows the different approaches and motives on a continuum. Figure 5.1 shows a very broad understanding of CSR, where each approach represents a categorization under which a number of theories are attached. The main discussion considers whether these motives behind CSR initiatives are profit or ethics oriented, or somewhere in between. Figure 5.1 also addresses the discussion regarding the reach of responsibility. That is, whether a given company's responsibility includes its shareholders, the stakeholders or the whole of society.

*Figure 5.1: Continuum of Motives for Responsible Conduct*

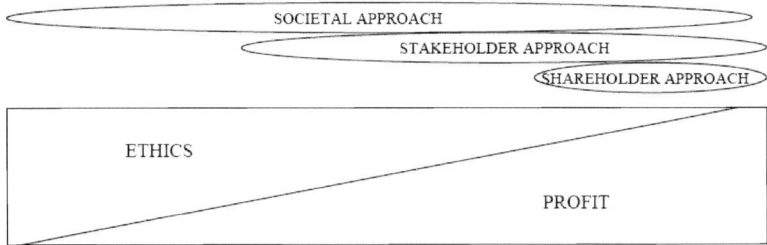

Source: van Liempd (2007, p. 33)

Several organizations have set up different standards for businesses to follow as guidelines for their work with CSR. One of these organizations is the UN, whose Global Compact guidelines consist of ten principles within the areas of human rights, labor standards, the environment and anti-corruption.

## UN Global Compact

The UN Global Compact program is a strategic policy initiative for businesses, which attaches high importance to aligning corporate strategies and operations with these ten widely accepted principles (www.unglobal-compact.org). Table 5.1 lists the principles within the four main categories.

The ten principles have contributed to framing the research questions and therefore, also the following empirical section. The main emphasis of this chapter is not on general theory, but on the exploratory case observations and interview results. The following empirical section is set forth in paradoxes, through which the theory on CSR will be reflected in an Indian context. The literature review, which has not been formulated explicitly in the theoretical section, will thus appear throughout the text in the empirical section.

*Table 5.1: UN Global Compact Principles*

| Human Rights | |
|---|---|
| Principle 1: | Businesses should support and respect the protection of internationally proclaimed human rights |
| Principle 2: | make sure that they are not complicit in human rights abuses |
| **Labor Standards** | |
| Principle 3: | Businesses should uphold the freedom of association and the effective recognition of the right to collective bargaining |
| Principle 4: | The elimination of all forms of forced and compulsory labor |
| Principle 5: | The effective abolition of child labor |
| Principle 6: | The elimination of discrimination in respect of employment and occupation |
| **Environment** | |
| Principle 7: | Businesses should support a precautionary approach to environmental challenges |
| Principle 8: | Undertake initiatives to promote greater environmental responsibility |
| Principle 9 | Encourage the development and diffusion of environmentally friendly technologies |
| **Anti-Corruption** | |
| Principle 10: | Businesses should work against corruption in all its forms, including extortion and bribery |

Source: www.unglobalcompact.org

Overall, the literature review is applied to gain an insight into the Indian understanding of CSR. In the empirical section, the literature review will be used to support the results. Provided that there exist conflicting elements from the literature compared with the results based on the empirical data of this exploratory case study, this will be accentuated.

## Empirical Data: CSR Paradoxes

This section contains the empirical results of the field study, which are composed of six paradoxes. Even though the paradoxes are discussed separately, they cannot always be viewed in isolation, as the paradoxes affect one another. The paradoxes are based primarily on the experiences from India and the UN Global Compact Principles. The different paradoxes are placed in an intuitive logical order. The paradoxes are listed in Table 5.2:

*Table 5.2: CSR Paradoxes in India*

| 1. Karma | vs. | Caste |
|---|---|---|
| 2. Philanthropy | vs. | Embedded in strategy |
| 3. Global | vs. | Local adaptation |
| 4. Official CSR-policy | vs. | Multitude of programs |
| 5. Own workforce | vs. | Outside agency employees |
| 6. Bribery | vs. | Anti-bribery |

Source: Own compilation

The following sections will elucidate each paradox. Each section has the same structure: a notion clarification, followed by a discussion of theory and empirical data.

## Paradox 1: Karma vs. Caste

This section will focus on the karma versus caste paradox. The paradox is that the belief in karma urges Indians to do good deeds, but at the same time social imbalances and injustices through the Indian caste system are generally accepted. There is a clear connection between karma and the caste system. The connection must be found in the belief in reincarnation. The soul is immortal, while the body is subject to birth and death. Thus, the caste Indians are born into is a result of karma from previous lives – generally speaking, as you sow, so shall you reap (Flood, 1996, p. 6).

In spite of the above mentioned connection between karma and the caste system, this section will at first discuss the notions separately. The understanding of the two notions is fundamental for the understanding of the paradox. Subsequently, the paradox will be discussed in relation to the CSR perspective focusing on the cultural differences between India and Denmark regarding business issues.

### Karma

In Hinduism, karma is one of the most fundamental doctrines. Karma means "deed" or "act" and encompasses, more broadly, the universal principle of cause and effect, action and reaction that governs all life (ibid.). Karma is determined by the intentions of the act, not the consequences of the act. If the intentions are good, the soul will improve. Karma is in that way a principle that describes how thoughts, words and actions create mental impressions. These impressions mature under the right circumstances, which will appear as outer or inner experiences. Whether these experiences are negative or positive depend on the good versus bad balance of karma. In that way, Hinduism has a very strict code of conduct

128

regarding behavior of life. A moral life and the acceptance of the given life situation are required (ibid., 55).

In broad outline, karma can be seen as an Eastern contradistinction to the Western concept of fate. One significant difference is that with karma it is to some extent possible to determine one's destiny. Bad karma makes one miserable and is followed by suffering and pain, while good karma brings happiness, prosperity and makes for an easy life. At the Day of Judgment, the karma accumulated during the most recent life and past lives is sized up and determines the status of the next life. Good karma elevates one to a higher caste in the next life, bad karma into a lower caste, while worst karma into an "untouchable" – which is the lowest possible caste, or actually the casteless, which are called Dalits (ibid., 59; 219). In Hinduism, there are three kinds of Karma, which are shown in Table 5.3 below:

*Table 5.3: Three Types of Karma in Hinduism*

| Type of Karma | Description |
| --- | --- |
| Sanchita karma | the total sum of past karmas yet to be resolved |
| Prarabdha karma | the portion of sanchita karma that is to be experienced in current life |
| Kriyamana karma | the karma that is created in the current life, which will bear fruit in the future – in current life or next |

Source: Own compilation, based on Sivananda (1999, p. 47)

Table 5.3 shows karma as an endless cycle. Sanchita karma is the accumulated karma from all previous lives. The ripe portion of this karma will be drawn out to serve one lifetime and is called the prarabdha karma – the fruit-bearing karma. It cannot be avoided or changed; it is only exhausted by being experienced. Kriyamana karma is the karma produced in the current life, and it will to some extend affect the current life. The rest of the kriyamana karma flows into sanchita karma and consequently shapes the future of next lives (Sivananda 1999, p. 47).

Critics may argue that the belief in karma is only a suitable explanatory model for higher cast members, in the way that the theory of karma legitimizes the cast system's social structure.

## Caste

The Indian Caste System describes the social stratification and the social restrictions of Indian society. In India, a caste is a hereditary social class in a traditionally and rigidly stratified society. One is born into a cast and social mobility is minimal (Fuller, 2004, p. 14). In Hinduism, a person's membership of a caste is of great importance and the castes are understood to be divinely determined. Other Indian religious movements, such as Buddhism and Sikhism are characterized by rejecting the caste system and thereby appealing to members of the lower castes. According to Indian tradition, to live ethically is to fulfill one's caste obligations (Flood, 1996, p. 55).

The Indian caste system is originally divided into four castes (*Varnas*), which are understood as an ideological setting for society (Fuller, 2004, p. 14). The four castes are designated as the *Brahmins* (priests, teachers and scholars), the *Kshatriyas* (rulers and warriors), the *Vaishyas* (landowners, traders and agriculturists) and the *Shudras* (service providers and artisans). In addition to these four groups, there is a group of casteless people, who bury bodies, sort rubbish e.g. People in this group are placed so low in the caste system, that they are not even mentioned in the old religious works (ibid., 15). Figure 5.2 gives an overview of the Varna system.

*Figure 5.2: The Indian Caste System*

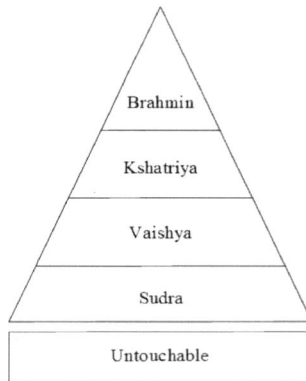

Brahmin

Kshatriya

Vaishya

Sudra

Untouchable

Source: Own compilation based on
Fuller (2004, p. 14)

The Varna system, as described above, shapes the overall system for the population, while later the *Jati*-system has been integrated. The Jati-system is a more fine-meshed system than the Varna system (religion.dk). While the Varnas make up the caste system's ideological frame, the Jatis make up the empirical reality. In India, there are about 3.000 different castes/Jatis (ibid.). An individual is born into a specific Jati and marriage is usually within the Jati. The Jati constitutes a closed social group, which has a common occupation and common rituals. In addition, within the Jatis, there is a group of seniors, who can punish members of the Jatis, who do not live up to internal caste duties (ibid.). One of the advantages of such a system is a clear division of labor and a strong feeling of belonging. However, while many Indians enjoy the fruits of the IT revolution, economic growth, and so on, the lower casts and the casteless are living in forced labor and oppression (Thorat, 2002, p. 572). Generally, casteless people are not allowed in temples and public places and in some areas, they are not even allowed to enter towns. The further away from the cities, the more pronounced the Indian caste system will be (ibid.). This is due to the fact that in the populous cities, it is too difficult to keep the various casts separated.

Critics may argue that the Indian caste system can be characterized as the biggest apartheid and slavery system in the world. Thorat (2002, p. 578) argues that unless the inequalities imbedded in the social, economic and cultural structure of society are not addressed, legal measures will make much less difference in providing basic human rights to the untouchables in India. In this relation, it should be mentioned, that the Indian government tries to remedy the situation through diverse measures, including positive discrimination through quotas in jobs and education. The situation has improved during the last decades, for example inter-caste marriages are now relatively common (filipspagnoli.wordpress.com). Unfortunately, the caste system remains deeply entrenched in Hindu culture and the improvements are not radical enough – it is hard to change a culture's ingrained mentality.

To a Westerner, it is difficult to understand how Indian society is structured and operates. The karma concept is at first very appealing and seems like a wonderful principle, but unfortunately, on the reverse side of the picture, there is a more serious and gloomy side. The caste system is cf. the Indian constitution officially abolished, but is so deeply embedded in Indian culture that it is impossible to remove completely. The interesting point of this paradox is what influence it has, when doing business in India regarding CSR issues. Is it possible to transfer the karma concept from the private sphere to the business sphere? And what does it mean for businesses that find themselves in a society which is largely dominated by a rigid stratified social structure?

Overall, Indian society is based on very different principles and beliefs than Western societies, and India is at a substantially lower development stage. Consequently, a Western understanding of CSR is difficult to transfer to the Indian culture. In India, for example, social imbalances are perceived as generally acceptable, and a traditional ethical life is lived by fulfilling caste obligations. Thus, something unethical in a Western sense may be ethical in the Indian sense. This puts demands on management for Danish companies in India. If the Western ethical framework is sought transferred, the Indians' understanding thereof cannot be taken for granted by management. This aspect refers to the paradox: global vs. local adaptation.

The visited subsidiaries were asked directly whether the belief in karma and reincarnation plays a role in how CSR is viewed in India. The question seemed difficult to answer. Maybe it is because karma is measured at the private individual level, which makes the concept not directly transferable to business issues. The subsidiaries' answers were therefore not very clear on the subject. Nevertheless, some indicators where found pointing in the direction of karma having a role regarding business conduct. Firstly, the private sphere and business sphere are not as separate as in Western societies. For instance, generally every meeting starts with a conversation regarding issues of private character, such as children, spouse and personal interests. After this, the subject of the meeting will be dealt with. Another indicator is the arguments used for explaining the motives behind CSR initiatives. Several of the subsidiaries stated that their CSR initiatives came from the heart not the brain. This is comparable to the theory of karma and indicates some kind of connection.

Karma is embedded in Indian culture and it can therefore be difficult to assess the true role of karma regarding CSR. It is an Indian tradition that companies donate money to temples and support various community activities (Chahoud et al., 2007, p. 3). This tradition can be traced back to ancient Indian kings and may therefore be rooted in religious beliefs, like karma. Chahoud et al. (2007, p. 30) state that Indian companies' current understanding of CSR is shaped primarily by the long Indian tradition of CSR and not by such global initiatives as e.g. the UN Global Compact.

If the caste system is viewed in a CSR perspective, caste membership could be having an impact on how employees are treated and which personnel are recruited. Most, if not all, respondents stated that they do not discriminate against employees on the basis of caste. Given the social structure of Indian society, this assertion is blurred, because the companies are hiring on the basis of education and skills, which are primarily found in certain casts. In India, it is mainly caste and parents, who decide their children's occupation – not as in Western society, where people become what they are passionate about or have talent for. This is an important point, since a policy not to discriminate against caste is then losing its substance. Equally, this issue will be highlighted by this chapter's own workforce vs. outside agency employees paradox. In this aspect, the subsidiaries discriminate, depending on the task or function of the individuals in the organization.

Slight discrimination was however also noted. For instance, it was several times noted that lower service personnel was subject to tougher talk from top management than middle managers. There were often several employees present only to keep track of the technical conditions for business presentations. Equally, tensions could be felt, when smaller technical problems arose. Considering these aspects and the general impression, the hierarchical structure must be considered as very strict and stratified, also in companies. The results of Hofstede's (1997) research also emphasize this impression through a relatively high score in the Indian power distance dimension. Perhaps these indicators can partly be explained by the stratified social structure in Indian society.

## Paradox 2: Philanthropy vs. Embedded in Strategy

This paradox is about how CSR is considered strategically, where the two extremes are philanthropy and embedded in strategy. This section will briefly introduce the two different approaches, whereupon the connection between the visited subsidiaries and the approaches will be discussed.

The philanthropic approach has its basis in charity, humanity and in things being performed by and with a good heart. Both charity and philanthropy can be regarded as sponsoring. Charity is understood as consisting solely of donations of money, whereas philanthropy includes the practical involvement of businesses (Chahoud et al., 2007, p. 26). CSR actions and initiatives within the philanthropic approach are taken "after the fact"; hence companies are responsible by giving something back to the society, after making money. That is, the company reactively sets up ad hoc projects to handle activities, while practical involvement is not part of routine operations. The philanthropic approach is characterized by having no specific strategic objective, which signifies that the approach is relatively simple with more short term engagement.

The embedded in strategy approach is characterized by CSR initiatives being a part of overall corporate strategy. That is, the initiatives create value in term of achieving strategic objectives. In this approach, the action is taken "before the fact"; that is, a company is proactively responsible towards society, while making money. That is, for instance, the involvement in philanthropic initiatives is implemented in routine processes of the organization and with a long term engagement. Within the embedded in strategy approach, CSR initiatives are very deliberate and strategic. The initiatives are not randomly selected, but selected and planed in alignment with corporate strategy. Table 5.4 illustrates the two notions of this paradox.

*Table 5.4: Paradox 2*

| Philanthropy | Embedded in Strategy |
|---|---|
| After the fact | Before the fact |
| Reactive | Proactive |
| No specific strategic objectives | Aligned with corporate objectives |
| Simple | Deliberate |
| Ad hoc | Routine operations |
| Short term engagement | Long term engagement |

Source: Own compilation

Philanthropic initiatives can be used to avoid opposition and protest from the company's local community. It is expected by Indian society that companies donate money to support development projects (Sagar and Singla, 2004, p. 285). For a company to obtain respect in India, including CSR aspects, it is not enough to be impressive with respect to financial results. Companies are not respected in India because they are powerful regarding financial results, they must in addition be transparent, have fair HR guidelines, contribute to society and be ethical (ibid.). Locals expect to get something in return for the companies' 'license to operate' in their community. Furthermore, by supporting the community, companies keep the cost of engagement within reasonable bounds (Chahoud et al., 2007, p. 69).

Support of the community can also be seen in light of the Indian tradition. Companies continue to feel a strong responsibility to give something back to the community, both in the form of charitable work and in financial support (Chahoud et al., 2007, p. 29). These traditions demand that companies to some extent make use of the philanthropy approach. In practice, a company's approach is often connected with the development stage of society. In India, philanthropy plays a great role, whereas in Denmark there is a social safety net, and societal support does thereby not have the same importance. However, Chapple and Moon (2005, p. 437) emphasize that the development stage of society is not the key factor to describe the Indian approach of CSR, compared to peer countries, such as Indonesia, South Korea and Singapore. Factors of historical and traditional nature have greater importance. These factors are associated with long-standing, religiously derived, philanthropic traditions, earlier epochs of the internationalization of business, colonization, and imperialism (ibid.).

134

The philanthropic importance for society was discussed at one of the visited subsidiaries. The respondents argued that it is easy to have success with a philanthropic approach in India, because of the lack of a social safety net. Plus the relative ease of showing commitment to the community with the use of a philanthropic approach. Whether the subsidiary's arguments have anything to do with how the CSR-strategy has emerged may be considered. Is the strategy dictated from Denmark or is it a result of local initiatives? This is also with reference to the global vs. local adaptation paradox.

The majority of the visited subsidiaries presented their CSR approach as an approach with a basis in philanthropy. Some of the subsidiaries accentuated the initiatives they have made to involve employees in their CSR tasks. These subsidiaries focused on motivating their employees to spend time doing voluntary work to support charitable purposes. In particular, the statement: "CSR is driven by the heart, not the brain", made by a manager in one of the subsidiaries symbolizes the philanthropic approach taken by many companies operating in India. This is also reflected by the fact that several of the subsidiaries did not consider it appropriate to discuss their CSR activities in public. They stated that had they not been asked, they would not have mentioned CSR in connection with the company presentation.

The philanthropic approach expressed itself through different community development programs, which were initiated reactively and mostly not aligned with corporate objectives. This observation is in line with Balasubramanian et al. (2005, p. 90) who state that many Indian companies are following a reactive mode. In this connection, it should be mentioned that one of the visited subsidiaries, besides supporting CSR initiatives outside their strategic area, also supported initiatives aligned with overall corporate strategy.

Empirical indicators for an embedded in strategy approach were very limited. However, one example should be given. A couple of the visited subsidiaries had a Green Building certificate, proving that the company is environmentally conscious, and performing within certain set environmental limits with regards to e.g. waste, energy, and water use. Actions such as painting the roofs white, energy-saving architecture and power from wind turbines are among the initiatives to acquire certification. It was in both cases only the administration building though, which had this certificate. It may be questioned whether this initiative is embedded in strategy, and furthermore if the focus on sustainability in *administration* makes a difference compared to for instance sustainability in *production*.

The above mentioned example may be interpreted as using a certificate to improve both the company's image and to legitimize its presence towards stakeholders. Sagar and Singla (2004, p. 285) indicate that Indian companies are moving away from being self-regulating to multi-stakeholder initiatives. Through the latest decades, stakeholders have gained a higher importance and influence on CSR in India (Chahoud et. al., 2007, p. 17). However, self-regulation is still profound and among others reflected in the limited co-operation with unions and socially orientated organizations, which leads them to not taking part in the shaping of the Indian CSR agenda (ibid.). In this relation, it should however be mentioned that a couple of the visited subsidiaries did consult with NGOs.

## Paradox 3: Global vs. Local Adaptation

This section will deal with the paradox of using either a global or a local CSR-strategy in India. The choice of strategy will in this section be discussed in relation to different levels of local adaptation. It is important to emphasize that this section focuses on the relation between corporate headquarters and the subsidiary. This entire case study concerns only Danish corporate headquarters and subsidiaries located in India.

The use of a global CSR-strategy means that all CSR-activities are initiated and controlled by corporate headquarters. This means that each subsidiary has to follow the policies and guidelines dictated from group headquarters. Thus, they have a global code of conduct, which outlines the possibilities the subsidiaries have for CSR-activities.

A local CSR-strategy means that corporate headquarters gives its subsidiaries latitude to decide, which CSR-activities to implement. This means that each subsidiary has to complete their own plan of CSR-activities and that they do not have to follow any restrictions given from the headquarters of the company.

In between the paradox of whether to have a global or a local CSR-strategy, there are different levels of local adaptation. Some headquarters hand policies and guidelines to its subsidiaries. Afterwards, it is up to the subsidiaries to adapt the policies and guidelines to the local circumstances. Although, the subsidiary has adopted its own CSR-strategy, it is still a possibility that company headquarters forces the business departments to report all CSR-activities. Table 5.5 illustrates this paradox and includes different levels of CSR-strategies.

*Table 5.5: Paradox 3*

| Level of Adaptation | Label | Policies | Systems | Outcomes |
|---|---|---|---|---|
| Level 3 | Global | HQ | HQ | HQ |
| Level 2 | Global | HQ | HQ | Local |
| Level 1 | Local | HQ | Local | Local |
| Level 0 | Local | Local | Local | Local |

Source: Own compilation

Whether headquarters or the subsidiary chooses to implement a global, local, or a CSR-strategy that is in between these two, plays a significant role with regard to the three topics in Table 5.5. As an extension to the text above, choosing a global CSR-strategy means that company headquarters dictates how the subsidiary's policies, systems and outcomes must be handled. On the other hand, having a local CSR-strategy implies that the subsidiary autonomously handles the CSR-policies, -systems and -outcomes.

The third column in Table 5.5 is policies. A well-known example of a global CSR-policy is the UN Global Compact as mentioned in the theory section. The UNGC is a strategic policy initiative for companies that want to be committed to aligning their operations and strategies with ten universally accepted principles.

The next column in Table 5.5 is systems. An example of a CSR-system is the International Organization for Standardization (ISO) standard 14000. With a network of national standard institutes in 162 countries and with more than 17.500 certificates, ISO is the world's largest developer and publisher of international standards. Two of the main areas of ISO-certificates are quality management systems and environmental management systems (www.iso.org).

Outcome is the last column in Table 5.5 and relates to the reporting of outcomes from CSR-activities. There are a lot of different standards for reporting, for instance, the network-based organization Global Reporting Initiative (Welford, 2004, p. 35). This organization has pioneered the development of the world's most widely used sustainability reporting framework.

Among others on the basis of the above mentioned characteristics in the paradox philanthropy versus embedded in strategy, there is a major difference in the way India and Denmark work with CSR-strategies. The difference between the Danish and the Indian way of working with CSR-strategies is among others rooted in legislation. According to the Danish

137

Financial Statement Act § 99a, Danish companies, in classification C or D (Danish Financial Statement Act § 7), are required to complement the management report with a statement of social responsibility. It means that companies voluntarily integrate areas such as human rights, social relationship, environmental and climatic conditions as well as fighting corruption in their business strategy and operations. The statement must contain information as required in Table 5.6.

*Table 5.6: Extract of Danish Financial Statement Act § 99a*

| |
| --- |
| 1) The policies of the business on social responsibility, including any standards, guidelines or principles for social responsibility that the business is using; |
| 2) How the business realizes its policies in social responsibility, including any systems or procedures in this respect; |
| 3) Assessment of the business on achievements resulting from its work on social responsibility in the financial year, and any future expectation to work of the business. |

Source: EOGS, p. 1

If companies have no policies of social responsibility, it should be disclosed in the management report. Compared with Danish legislation, the Trade Council of Denmark in India states that India only has minimum environmental and labor laws, which do not contain any restrictions or information regarding CSR-activities and reporting. In this relation, it should be mentioned that the referred part of the Danish legislation first took effect in 2009.

A significant part of the visited subsidiaries have a local CSR-strategy. Approximately half of these have a global code of conduct, which is adapted to local circumstances. The other half of the subsidiaries has no guidelines from Danish headquarters. Therefore, it is the local companies own decision, which activities they attend to.

A modest part of the subsidiaries are working under a global code of conduct, which means that guidelines are given from Denmark. These guidelines have to be strictly followed by the Indian subsidiary. As an example, one of the visited subsidiaries had very specific guidelines from headquarters regarding CSR-activities that needed to be carried out and reported back on. Chapple and Moon (2005, p. 430) portray India as the country that most extensively reports its CSR, compared with peer countries. However, the observations made in the present study are not in agreement with this, because CSR reporting was hardly found. Furthermore,

138

it should be mentioned that companies designated as international are more likely to report their CSR than those designated as domestic (ibid., p. 438).

Prieto-Carrón et al. (2006, p. 982) are skeptical and see limitations of relying on codes of conduct in the case of India. It is argued that international companies, instead of assisting their suppliers to improve their social and environmental performance by providing incentives or sharing the cost of improvement, are simply moving to those suppliers which fulfill some of their social and environmental criteria (ibid.). These criteria are predominantly ISO standards (ISO 14001, ISO 9000, ISO 18001) or some labor standard. Prieto-Carrón et al. (2006, p. 982) only see very little improvement in social and environmental performance, while the systems often squeeze the already low margins of their suppliers.

This paradox regarding global versus local adaptation can partly be explained by the Indian culture's use of philanthropy. Most of the visited subsidiaries state that CSR-initiatives come from the heart instead of the brain. This could indicate that Indians are much more interested in, and pay more attention to, the Indian community and its welfare, instead of aligning the initiatives with corporate objectives.

Another remarkable answer to the fact that a significant part of the subsidiaries use an adapted CSR-strategy rather than a global is that there is a major difference in the two countries traditions and stages of development. The difference in the stage of development also signifies a difference in relation to the legislation regarding CSR in respectively Denmark and India.

## Paradox 4: Official CSR-Policy vs. Multitude of Programs

This paradox concerns the question whether a company has an official CSR-policy or has a multitude of CSR-programs. This section briefly introduces the two different notions and clarifies their differences. Subsequently, the experiences from India will be discussed and displayed in relation to the notions.

An official CSR-policy signifies that the company has an explicit, written policy regarding CSR. That is, the company acts on procedures and guidelines, when initiating CSR-activities. The word 'official' can in this context easily be misunderstood, signifying that the company acts in another way than proclaimed. This is not what is meant here; the word official only relates having *explicit* guidelines. These guidelines hold the given company's code of conduct and, to some extent, decision criteria for which CSR initiatives to launch. Official CSR-policies can be compared to a top-down

139

mindset, which is characterized by lines of direction given by top management.

A multitude of programs refer to initiated CSR-activities based on no official policies. These initiatives are more based on suddenly emerged opportunities, where the activities are chosen partly randomly on the basis of intuition. There are fewer guidelines, hardly written policies since the formalization is implicit; nevertheless CSR-activities are launched. In this notion, the accumulation of these activities is denoted as a multitude of programs. A bottom-up mindset is comparable with a multitude of programs, because the programs often are initiated on the operational level. Table 5.7 illustrates the characteristics of the two notions in this paradox.

*Table 5.7: Paradox 4*

| Offical CSR-policy | Multitude Programs |
|---|---|
| Guidelines | Intuition |
| Top-down | Bottom-up |
| Explicit formalisation | Implicit formalisation |
| Brain | Heart |

Source: Own compilation

The cultural differences between Denmark and India have a major impact on the understanding of CSR. In Denmark, CSR is characterized with a top-down approach, where CSR activities are explicitly formulated in policies. That is, Danish companies compose a lot of paperwork, but it can be questioned whether this work actually results in definite activities. In Denmark, CSR can be understood as a communication tool, which critics may see as risk management and manipulation in relation to stakeholders (Kolk and Pinkse, 2006, p. 62). In spite of this, companies with official CSR-strategies are better off if scandals occur, because they have a contingency plan, where the multitude of program approach does not have any strategic documents to use in defense.

This paradox must also be viewed in the light of the stage of development. For instance, in Denmark especially, the media pressures companies (Midttun et al., 2006, p. 375). In India, the situation is very different, because the development stage is significant lower and entirely different traditions exist. Problems are relative to the surrounding conditions. That is, the scale of problems related to society is relative to the scale of problems caused by companies in society. Therefore, Indian companies have more latitude to operate and receive less pressure from stakeholders and media. However, Indian society still expects larger companies to give something back to society, after the fact.

A significant part of the visited subsidiaries belong to the category of a multitude of programs. Several subsidiaries stated that the CSR initiatives were based on no specific decision criteria, and done from the heart. Instead, the initiatives were based on suddenly emerged opportunities. For instance, subsidiaries mentioned activities such as: teach small children to wash their hands correctly, support children at orphanages, and plant trees in the surrounding environment. These examples largely reflect that the activities are launched intuitively and not based on specific guidelines. Managers do not consider CSR initiatives in proportion to guidelines, but rather in relation to whether there is room in the budget, and if the initiative intuitively is a kind-hearted idea.

Nevertheless, a few of the subsidiaries used NGOs for advice regarding which activities to initiate. One subsidiary, for instance, supports an AIDS campaign, based on an NGO recommendation. This campaign is not due to any guidelines and could as well have been another campaign, because the decision was not based on any specific criteria.

The few subsidiaries, which have an official CSR-policy, have based their decisions regarding CSR initiatives on written guidelines from Denmark. However, these subsidiaries do not transfer and implement the CSR-policies to India without adding some Indian specific initiatives to the policies. The added initiatives do among other have basis in Indian culture. Indian culture is representative for low individualization (Hofstede, 1997), but attaches a high importance to protecting and taking care of people surrounding them. An example of this is reflected in some of the visited subsidiaries, where medical insurance is provided to both the employee and the employee's family. Hence, the subsidiaries in question do establish extra programs as a supplement to official policies transferred from Denmark.

To sum up, a significant part of the visited subsidiaries have a multitude of programs, while only a few have official CSR-policies. This is in line with a survey carried out in India in 2003. It was found that not even 20 percent of the large corporations surveyed had a policy or a formal programme on CSR, and of these, the majority was philanthropic in nature, involving tiny sums of money (Prieto-Carrón et al. 2006, p. 983). The part concerning tiny sums of money is also in agreement with the findings of the current study.

Chapple and Moon (2005, p. 432) state that the Indian way of working with CSR is systematic. This is in contrast with the findings of the current study. However, it should be noted, that the survey of Chapple and Moon

(2005) expounds CSR in Indian compared to peer countries, which make "systematic" relative – not absolute on a global scale.

**Paradox 5: Own Workforce vs. Outside Agency Employees**

This section will deal with the paradox of employing one's own workforce and hiring labor from outside agencies. The two different approaches will be introduced, whereupon the connection between the visited subsidiaries and the approaches will be discussed. It is important to emphasize that this paradox concerns the conditions of employment in the subsidiaries.

One's own workforce contains the group of employees that are paid by the company, where they execute tasks. These tasks primarily concern the company's specific main work areas. These employees can be considered professionals within these work areas. For instance, the company's own workforce is hired to maintain specific work areas such as production, sales, research and development and other company-specific areas. Since the employees are employed directly by the company, wage and insurance agreements generally surpass minimum labor laws, especially in large companies.

Outside agencies employees are characterized by the employees that are paid by outside agencies. These agencies are hired to provide staff for a given company's maintenance and internal service tasks. These employees can be considered menial and custodian workers, doing jobs such as cleaning, maintenance of outside areas, window washing or canteen operation, for example. These employees are hired under different conditions than the people working in the company in question. These conditions are often only in agreement with the minimum labor laws. Table 5.8 illustrates the two notions of the paradox.

*Table 5.8 Paradox 5*

| Own Workforce | Outside Agency Employees |
|---|---|
| Paid by the company | Paid by an agency |
| Primary operation | Maintenance and internal service |
| Professionals | Menial and custodian workers |
| Wage and insurance agreement | Minimum labor laws |

Source: Own compilation

Cultural and legislative aspects have a large influence on how this paradox is viewed. In Denmark, the gap between outside agencies and companies are relatively small with reference to conditions of employment. Compared to

Danish conditions, the Indian gap is considerable larger, because the minimum labor requirements are significantly lower than in Denmark. This is illustrated in Figure 5.3.

*Figure 5.3: Gap Between Internal Employee and Minimum Labor Laws*

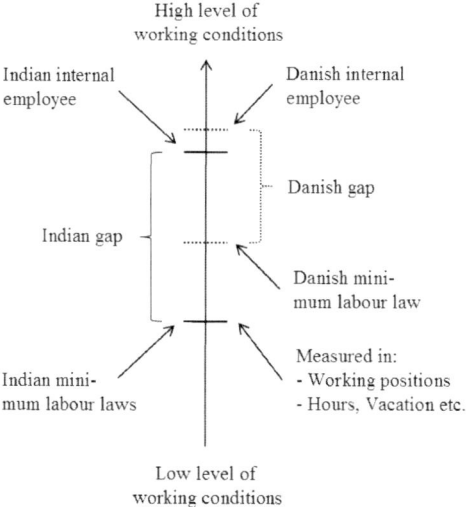

Source: Own compilation

The levels of minimum labor laws are measured by weekly working hours, working environment, vacation etc., while the levels of actual realized working conditions are set according to best judgment. For instance, the differences in weekly working hours are 48 hours in India compared to 37 hours in Denmark, while the differences according to vacation is respectively two weeks paid vs. seven weeks paid (www.csrkompasset.dk). However, it should be noted that minimum labor laws differ in Indian regions.

The Indian gap is also reflected in Indian culture, where differential treatment is generally accepted. This can be an explanation of why the Indian gap is larger than the Danish. Furthermore, it can be questioned to which extent the minimum labor laws are respected by outside agencies. Some examples indicate that these minimum labor laws are disrespected, because supervision is difficult. An example of this indication is that a company has an agreement with a security company. The security people have to work twelve hours a day for six days, and the last day of the week they work 24 hours, because they have to switch from day to night shift. Another example is that the lowest castes – the Dalits or Untouchables – regularly are refused payment in spite of that they have performed the work (www.csrkompasset.dk). In this relation, it should be mentioned that this was not experienced at any of the visited companies.

The Danish subsidiaries visited in India have taken different initiatives to help their own workforce. A large part of the visited subsidiaries have special health insurances for their workforce. The special thing in comparison to health insurances in Denmark is that the insurances often not only cover the employee, the spouse and the children, but also covers the employee's parents. Such social CSR initiatives seemed to be generally common in large companies.

While most of the subsidiaries visited offer health insurance for their own workforce, this is not the only initiative. Most of them help their employees. One subsidiary visited provides loans for employees to make it possible for them to have a better everyday life. The subsidiary also provides houses, to make sure that the employees have a proper place to live. These initiatives ensure that employees are being taking care of on a physical need level.

Another example is that one of the visited subsidiaries did, in addition to the health insurances, also offer the employees to be picked up by a bus in the morning and brought home after work in the evening. This is provided so that all employees without a car are able to get to work. And from the subsidiary's perspective, it makes it more likely that the employees are on time for work. Education and personal development are a focal issue for the same subsidiary, as well as for the parent company. A talent program is created to provide especially talented employees with extra education and personal growth by sending these employees to other departments in different countries.

All these initiatives that the visited subsidiaries are proud of doing for the employees are only available for their own workforce. As mentioned earlier, most of the subsidiaries have hired agencies to take care of cleaning, maintenance and other not company-specific jobs. These people are working under different circumstances compared to the own workforce. Because they are employed by an agency that is offering its services to the subsidiaries, the particular subsidiaries in which they are working do not feel any responsibility for the conditions they are working under. In other words the visited subsidiaries are generally disclaiming responsibility for the wellbeing of the service staff. It is notable that every time questions about the outside agencies employees were asked, the subsidiaries were dismissive of any kind of responsibility, as they did not recognize the topic as their field of responsibility.

In general, it seems that companies in India are very concerned about the wellbeing and good lives of their own workforce. Some go far in their attempt to help, where it is needed and where they can see it has meaning and an effect. However, this is only the case, when it comes to the company's own workforce. When it comes to the service help hired from outside agencies, there is generally no feeling of being responsible for their working conditions and their wellbeing. Consequently, nothing is actively done in order to help outside agency employees in any way, since the labor laws must be respected by the agency by which they are hired.

Whether or not the company has a responsibility to take care of the staff they employ from outside agencies can be discussed. The staff is employed under different circumstances, but since they are working for the particular company and performing jobs and tasks for the company, it could be argued that the company also has a responsibility to make sure that their working conditions are improved. By also taking a responsibility for the employees from outside agencies, the companies are showing that they are willing to take a bigger social responsibility. In connection to this, Prieto-Carrón et al. (2006, p. 986) state that India might see the CSR initiative ostensibly aimed at raising labor standards as a weakening factor regarding competitive position seen in a global scale. It is all about finding the right balance, which can be very difficult – especially when ethics are highly culturally determined.

## Paradox 6: Bribery vs. Anti-Bribery

This section introduces the paradox between bribery and anti-bribery. The two notions will be clarified separately, whereupon a brief discussion according to the visited subsidiaries will follow.

Bribery constitutes a crime and is defined by Black's Law Dictionary as the offering, giving, receiving or soliciting of any item of value to influence the actions of an official or other person in discharge of a public or legal duty. The bribe is the gift bestowed to influence the recipient's conduct. It may be any money, good, right in action, property, preferment, privilege, emolument, object of value, advantage, or merely a promise or undertaking to induce or influence the action, vote, or influence of a person in an official or public capacity.

Anti-bribery is best described as a clear choice not to engage in using bribery. The OECD has made an anti-bribery convention that is establishing legally binding standards to criminalize bribery of foreign public officials in international business transactions (www.oecd.org). It is no longer possible for a company to get tax deductibility for bribes paid to foreign officials, in any of the 38 countries that take part in the convention. Denmark is one of the 38 participating countries, while India is not. However, the rules in the convention also apply to Danish companies that have departments in other countries.

Bribery is a problem in a lot of countries. Companies are sometimes forced to use bribery in order to get their activities to go faster and smoother. Since bribery is practically nonexistent, and illegal, in Denmark, most companies will be unwilling to use bribery in other parts of the world, because it goes against the morality of the company. Table 5.9 illustrates the characteristics of the two notions in this paradox.

Even though bribery is said to be an unaccepted part of doing business in India, a look at the Corruption Perceptions Index (CPI) shows that bribery is much more used than claimed. In the CPI from 2009, India is placed on a shared 84th place on a list with 180 countries. India has a score of 3.4 out of 10 possible, where 10 is the best (transparency.org). One of the visited subsidiaries explained that corruption in India was much worse ten years ago. This is correct, but corruption is still a relatively big problem in India, seen in a global context.

*Table 5.9: Paradox 6*

| Claims | Practice |
|---|---|
| High moral | "Greasing money" |
| Official anti-bribery policy | Policies not respected |
| Talking the talk | Not walking the walk |

Source: Own compilation

Another example of the existence of bribery in India can be seen going through advertisements from different lawyers. In the advertisements, lawyers accentuate their expert knowledge within the area (www.hg.org). However, in the advertisements, it is not emphasized, whether the lawyers help companies use bribery or if they specialize in protecting companies against bribery and helping them judicially subsequently. Besides elucidating the problem, this is also an indication of the uncertainty regarding the actual extent of bribery – if several lawyers specialize in bribery, then it must exist.

Several of the visited subsidiaries in India stated that they do not use bribery nor take bribery from others. One subsidiary stated that it makes it very clear to new employees that bribery is not an accepted part of business operations. Instead, employees are instructed in what to do if they are in a position, where bribery is offered or demanded.

Even though most companies refuse to be users of bribery, there are unfortunately strong incentives for using it anyway. India is a large democracy and a very bureaucratic country. This means that a lot of things can take long time to get permissions for. At the same time, there are a lot of companies trying to get the same orders. Bribery can therefore make the bureaucratic process go faster and perhaps ensure that the company is getting the specific order that they were hoping to get. Prieto-Carrón et al. (2006, p. 978) are very direct concerning the aspect of corruption in India. They state that in India, it is the rule rather than the exception that companies do not comply with existing legal frameworks related to corruption, payment of taxes, fair trade practices, respect for human rights, customer services, and environmental protection. The challenge in India is first to get business to meet these basic legal obligations (ibid.). This statement was not possible to validate, but the general impression of the visited subsidiaries do not support this statement. There are of course disadvantages in connection with bribery. Danish companies are not in the habit of using bribery in their home country, and bribery is not positively looked upon. By using bribery in their foreign subsidiaries, it can cause serious damage to their reputation in Denmark. Clearly, no company is interested in ruining its reputation, and engaging in bribery must be carefully considered and officially dissociated oneself from.

## Conclusion

This conclusion contains a summary, managerial recommendations and a final perspective. The summary is intended to answer the main research question: *How is CSR considered in India?* The recommendations are intended to give directions to foreign companies – especially Danish companies – who contemplate doing business in India. Beyond this, the recommendations can be applied by both theorists and practitioners, who wish insight in the subject. The final perspective seeks to illustrate, which learning aspects Western companies can draw from the Indian way of doing business regarding CSR issues.

### Summary

CSR in India is not characterized by a focus on the environment, but by a social focus, mostly within the philanthropic approach. Equally, the CSR approach in India is characterized by few guidelines and very limited explicit and official policies. This approach must be seen in the light of a very stratified society, a relatively low stage of development and ingrained philanthropic traditions. Regarding the Indian approach in connection to the UN Global Compact ten principles, the visited companies expressed an orientation towards the social aspects of CSR. CSR initiatives are often in the form of different philanthropic initiatives, where projects in the local community are supported or initiated. The Indian tradition has historical roots, where it is expected that larger companies give back to society after the fact of making money.

## Managerial Recommendations

The focus in Indian companies is largely on external CSR activities, such as societal development initiatives. Instead, the companies should also focus on internal aspects, such as sustainable production. In this relation, it is important to emphasize that the visited subsidiaries also focused on internal aspects regarding social initiatives.

The ten principles from the UN Global Compact can be used as a framework or as a code of conduct, when doing business in India. Furthermore, the CSR policy should be more explicitly written and the initiatives can with advantage be aligned with corporate objectives. Below, a list of recommendations is formulated, for the purpose to advice companies considering doing business in India. These recommendations originate from the six paradoxes:

- Immerse in Indian cultural aspects, such as karma, caste and spirituality. These have great importance in the dynamics of Indian society.
- What is considered unethical in Denmark may be considered normal business practice in India.
- Be aware of discrimination and actively try to discourage it. Social stratification and restrictions in society also influence working conditions in business.
- First, initiate philanthropic activities to gain legitimacy, and try to align these with strategic objectives. Second, try to embed the initiatives into operations. Indian traditions and the development stage of society make demands for especially philanthropic initiatives.
- Implement philanthropic activities in collaboration with NGOs as these organizations are impartial and have expert knowledge on specific subjects.

- Move gradually towards global adaptation. There is a need for more guidelines in India, which leads to increased control, influence and decreases the risk of scandals.
- Pay attention to the gap between Indian minimum labor laws and the actual realized working conditions. This gap can be closed by not utilizing outside agency employees. The company can be held responsible towards stakeholders, media etc. if society is moving towards Western tendencies.
- Be aware of the relatively high level of corruption in India. Bribery is used to some extent in India, but it is not well-seen. Training of employees can in this relation help avoiding improper situations.

## Perspective

In relation to India and Western countries, it can be argued that the learning process goes both ways. Western countries' CSR-policies can be accused of being emotional detached. Where are the emotions and the enthusiasm in the Danish approach to CSR? It is almost too professional. Instead, Western countries should focus more on initiating CSR programs from the heart, which will increase enthusiasm and engagement in companies. A more ethical approach to CSR can maybe contribute to discovering new latent markets – creative and innovative processes should not be embedded in too strict managerial settings.

# CHAPTER 6

# Epilogue: Learning and Reflection

*Jan Stentoft Arlbjørn, Henning de Haas, Mads Bruun Ingstrup and Dennis van Liempd*

## Abstract

*This chapter summarizes and concludes on both the process, the results, and the technical and social learning elements for the participating students. It is based on the students' answers to an evaluating questionnaire. The chapter ends with extracting the overall conclusions for the four themes of the field study trip.*

## Introduction

This final chapter is a reflection on the course *International Field Studies* offered by the Department of Entrepreneurship and Relationship Management at the University of Southern Denmark in Kolding. In the course description the purpose of the course is stated as follows:

> *"To develop the students' skills in applying specific theories and approaches from a general ontological, epistemological and methodological perspective to a concrete business problem in collaboration with other students. Furthermore, the purpose is also for the students to obtain experience in acquiring the necessary technical, social and ethical competencies in conducting international field work."*

Thus, the aim of the course is to develop the students' skills in conducting all phases of a smaller field study, including the preparatory desk research, the organization of the field work, and the completion of subsequent analyses and reports.

On their last day in India, the students were asked to fill out a brief questionnaire in order to follow up on the purpose of this course. The questionnaire included eleven questions of which three were open questions allowing the students to reflect and comment on their experiences and learning. The rest of the questions were answered on a 7-point Likert scale (1 = low degree of agreement and 7 = high degree). All 22 enrolled students answered the eleven questions. The results of this survey are presented here, since they can provide learning to others. They might for example have interest for other persons in the process of planning or executing a similar course. Furthermore, since the composition of the course puts the students in close physical proximity to the core content of their theoretical studies, it can contribute to the continuous discussions on creating stimulating learning environments, also in courses of longer duration.

The chapter is organized in short sections, where the students' feedback on the most impressive experiences during the field study trip is presented. The chapter ends by presenting conclusions on the overall trip, and brief conclusions on the respective student chapters' findings.

## Most Impressive Experiences

The students were asked to reflect on and rank what had been the three most impressive experiences during the field study trip. The results are:

1. The gap between Danish and Indian culture.
2. The company visits including business understanding.
3. The social aspect of being together as a group and as tourists.

The students were asked to evaluate whether the course had given them a better understanding of relevant theories to be used to solve their research questions. The results of this question are shown in Figure 6.1.

*Figure 6.1: Better Understanding of Relevant Theories and Methods*

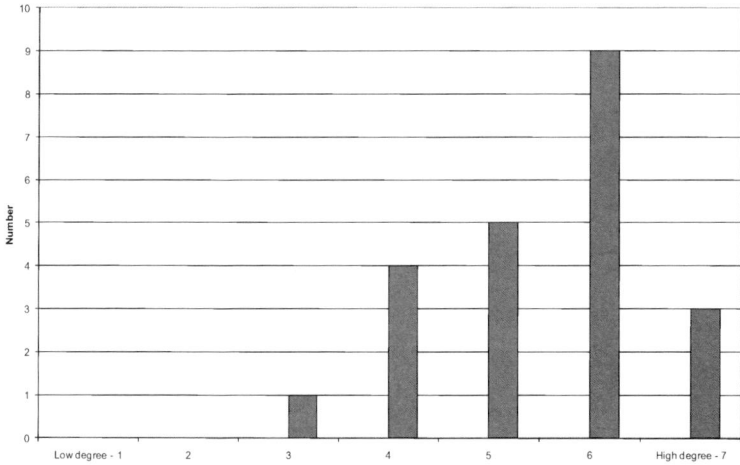

With an average score of 5.41 on a seven point scale, it can be concluded that the students feel they have obtained a better understanding of relevant theories and methods during the course. The close presence with the subject matter in India has given the students new understandings of theories and methods, and how to adjust these to other contexts beside a Western one. Thus, students should not only learn relevant theories, but they should also learn their limitations and how to apply them in practice.

## Application of Relevant Theories and Methods

The students were asked to evaluate the degree to which they were challenged in using relevant theories and methods in order to solve their research questions in their respective assignments. The result is illustrated in Figure 6.2.

153

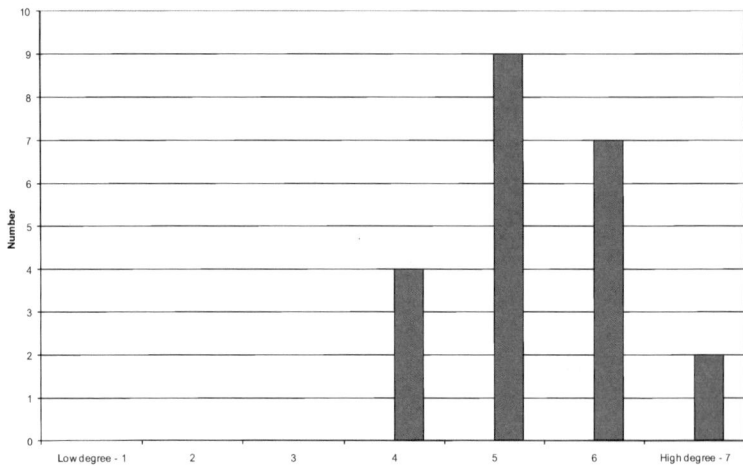

The result of this question indicates that the students feel they have been challenged by finding theories to be used in order to cover their research questions. The average is 5.31 on a seven point scale. As a general observation, it can be mentioned that all groups found themselves relatively confident with their theory selection before the actual field study trip. However, their stay in India with the interviews, observations and their presence in the culture provided them with a more nuanced view of theories and methods and how to apply these.

## Improved Competencies Through Group Work

The students were then asked to evaluate to which degree participation in the course had improved their competencies in conducting group work. Results to this question are shown in Figure 6.3.

*Figure 6.3: Improved Social Competencies Through Group Work*

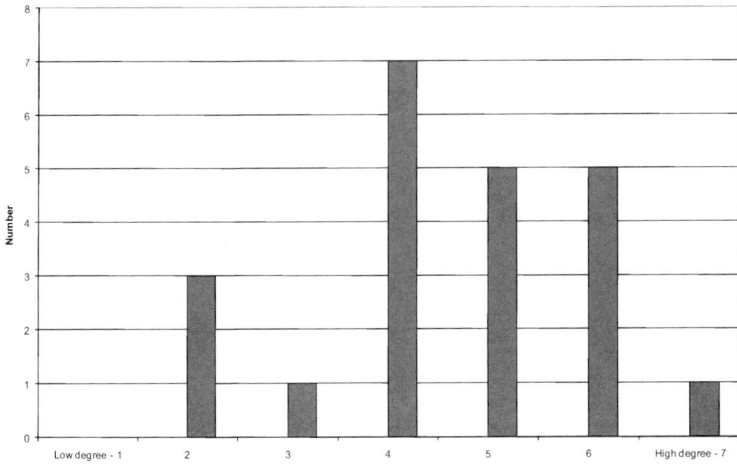

When looking at the answers, it seems that most of the students believe they have improved their social competencies with respect to group work from a medium to a high degree. The average score on this question is 4.50. At the time of evaluation, the students were still in the process of writing their assignments. To this point, they had mainly been working with theories and methods. Data analyses were just begun. Not all four groups worked alike. Some groups worked together in all aspects, while others divided the group into sub-groups with specific responsibilities.

## Better Understanding of Indian Culture

The students were additionally asked to reflect upon whether the field study trip had provided them with a better understanding of the Indian culture. The results can be seen in Figure 6.4.

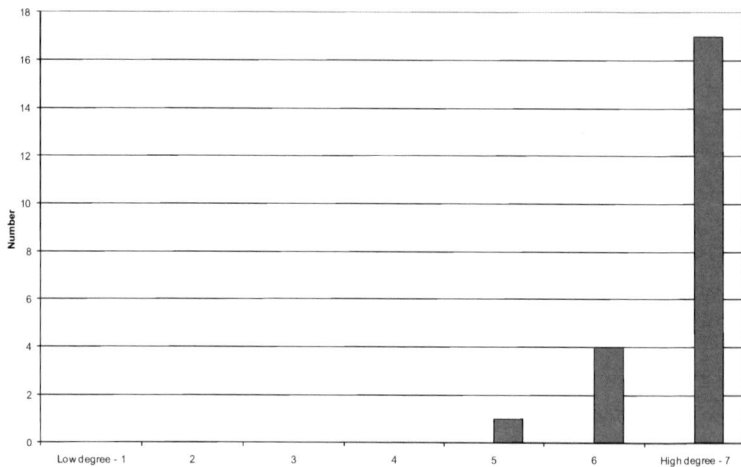

There is a significant indication that this field study trip has given the students a better and deeper insight into Indian culture and society. The average score on this question is 6.73. The companies visited excelled in including cultural aspects of doing business in India in their presentations and discussions. This has allowed the students to get first and second hand insights from people living in the culture. Together with actually being in Indian cities, this has given them much cultural learning and understanding.

## The Most Important Points of Cultural Learning

The students were asked what they perceived as the most giving cultural learning from the field study trip. The elements most often mentioned are summarized below.

- The different developmental stages in which India is growing
- The importance of meeting the basic needs of the population
- The harmony and spirituality in society
- The way relationships are built and maintained
- The caste system
- The sense of time in India (Indian Stretchable Time)
- The avoidance of saying no in order to maintain face and harmony
- The overcapacity of resources including people

# Conclusion

This book is titled Supply Chain Management: Business Operations in India. This theme has been chosen due to its practical relevance in the present time, where countries and companies more than ever are building relationships across borders. The global economy is becoming more complex through global sourcing and trade from all parts of the world. As a consequence, India both in terms of location for production and in terms of market penetration has been discussed widely. Therefore, outsourcing as well as localization and business clusters were issues considered to be central topics to investigate during the field study trip and thus also in this book. Due to increased business activity with Indian companies and Indian society, the concept of relationship management was considered important to study with a variety of issues relating to cultural differences and business practices. Finally, the concept of Corporate Social Responsibility (CSR) is a strategic element in many companies where many resources are invested, for example to secure that suppliers are not employing child labor at their facilities, that employees do not operate under dangerous and polluted working conditions or that suppliers do not underpay their employees. It was therefore a natural choice also to investigate CSR at the companies visited in India. In the following, conclusions on the research questions to each of the four themes are briefly provided.

## Outsourcing and Off-Shoring

Theoretical perspectives on outsourcing and off-shoring have been the point of reference for the research questions presented in this paragraph:

- What is the most common objective for initiating outsourcing/off-shoring of business processes to India?
- What is the nature of business processes performed by suppliers in India?
- What is the role of human capital factors in the location decision for companies' outsourcing/off-shoring business processes to India?
- Which location factors cause the most significant challenges for the BPO industry?

The first research question indicates that cost reduction is the most significant objective for foreign companies to move activities to India. Also, focus on core competences is becoming a more prevailing objective. In

157

relation to research question two, it was found that the type and complexity of the activities were important. The BPO industry in India started mainly by providing front-office activities, but has developed to also include back-office activities. Processes are still standardized, but on a higher level of expertise in areas such as finance, IT and legal services. Answering research question three, it was found that when moving business processes to India the most important human capital factors influencing the location decision were labor availability and quality of the workforce. A more challenging human capital factor discovered was the cultural distance, with issues regarding unwillingness to say no, failing to fulfill deadlines, the importance of establishing and maintaining relationships and the inability to think outside the box. Research question four covered the last factors influencing the location decisions including the problems regarding IT-infrastructure and power interruptions. Politically, the main problem is the widespread democracy in India, as democracy brings along very bureaucratic authorities.

## Business Clusters and Localization

In the chapter on business clusters and localization, the purpose was to identify and portray cluster activity in Southern India, and to discuss how Danish companies located in this particular area could benefit from their location. The following research question was asked:

- What can Danish companies learn from other company experiences about location and cluster participation in Southern India?

The study concludes that not all of the companies visited were familiar with the term business cluster even though some of them were located in one, which was influencing their business operations and strategy. Other companies considered their particular location less significant for the activities carried out. The choice of location among the visited companies were motivated and influenced by a number of different factors such as the infrastructure, the accessibility of skilled labor, suppliers' and competitors location, labor laws with particular focus on wages, prices on land etc. These factors have different levels of importance for each company, where some have more relevance than others. Furthermore the research findings stress that, depending on which industry companies are located in, it can be beneficial to explore ways of clustering in Southern India. However, localization in Southern India and participating in cluster activities should only be recommended if these activities contribute to value creation with regard to company output as a whole.

## Relationship Management

The aim of the relationship management chapter was to get a deeper understanding of issues having an impact on the way business is done in India. The chapter set out to answer three questions on how relationship management is carried out in India between companies and their customers.

- Which cultural issues impact the way of doing business in India?
- Which environmental factors impact Indian business? (in terms of political, economical, social, technological and legal factors)
- How is relationship management used in an Indian context?

With respect to question one, many *cultural issues* impact the way of doing business in India. First of all, personal relationships with those you are doing business with are very important. Secondly, the caste system affects the way of communicating, in that Indians have different privileges depending on status. It is therefore important that you are at the same level. Thirdly, in India, there is a massive focus on 'future orientation' which Western companies can benefit from. Fourth, Indians seem to be open to conduct business and retain knowledge from the West. Lastly, Indian companies are more hierarchical and employees do not express themselves as openly and directly as we do in the West. This also makes the ability to exercise control and provide direction one of the most important requirements when doing business in India.

There are also several *environmental factors* that impact doing business in India. Currently there is a huge growth in the middle class who have increasing purchasing power. Secondly, India is the world largest democracy, so everyone is allowed to have democratic opinions and go to court on contended issues. This can sometimes make the decision making process difficult and very slow. Therefore, plenty of time and manpower are needed when doing business in India. On the other hand, as mentioned, the caste system still exists which means that communication and decisions in general takes place between persons at same levels. Finally, India has labor laws protecting individuals' rights, including minimum wages and guarantees that a laborer after six months cannot be dismissed without a retirement benefit plan.

Concluding, it can be claimed that Indian companies always seek to build a *relationship* with other business partners, and they seem quick to adapt to relationship building behavioral strategies. The most common relational strategy used in India is "team selling".

## Corporate Social Responsibility

Corporate Social Responsibility (CSR) can have a multitude of different definitions, approaches, drivers and motivations, and can be practiced differently according to the developmental stages of the respective countries. Since there are large cultural and developmental differences between Denmark and India, the aim of the CSR chapter was to get a deeper understanding of how different views on CSR impact the way of doing business in India. It stands clear that the CSR focus in India is on the social aspect, while environmental aspects have a lesser focus.

The chapter gave rise to different paradoxes, which describe the CSR challenges that western companies can meet when doing business in India. These paradoxes also resulted in practical managerial implications.

Summing up, Indian society believes on the one hand in karma and doing good ethical deeds, while on the other hand this also results in the acceptance of the caste system, which suppresses people and their needs. Managers should be aware of these potential conflicts. Secondly, due to differences in developmental stages, Indian CSR approaches are often philanthropic in nature, with a focus on motives of a good heart and the right thing to do, while western approaches are beginning to be more embedded in strategy, with a focus on the financial bottom-line. Thirdly, as opposed to Danish headquarters, most Danish companies in India were not applying global CSR policies systems or outcome indicators, but were working with local, more ad-hoc strategies and guidelines. This potential mismatch is an issue to consider for management. Even though most Danish companies in India were not applying global guidelines given by headquarters, they did have a multitude of CSR programmes in place, often of a social nature. These seemed intuitive, bottom-up, and from the heart.

Concluding, it can be claimed that CSR in India is characterized by a multitude of different programmes motivated by a philanthropic approach from the heart, with few official, explicit or global guidelines and policies. It also focuses more on social than on environmental aspects, while cultural and spiritual factors influence the way CSR is seen and practised in a daily context.

# List of References

Adolphsen, G. (2004): *Indisk Kalejdoskop: Indien i dag*, Tiderne Skifter, København.

Andersen, I. (2005): *Den skinbarlige virkelighed – Vidensproduktion inden for samfundsvidenskaberne*, Forlaget Samfundslitteratur, Frederiksberg.

Arlbjørn, J.S. (2006): *Grundbog i Supply Chain Management*, Syddansk Universitetsforlag, Odense.

Arlbjørn, J.S. and de Haas, H. (eds.) (2009): *Supply Chain Management – Issues to Consider when Doing Business in China*, Academica, Aarhus.

Balasubramanian, N.K., Kimber, D. and Siemensma, F. (2005): "Emerging opportunities or traditions reinforced? an analysis of the attitudes towards CSR, and trends of thinking about CSR, in India", *Journal of Corporate Citizenship*, Vol. 17, No. 1, pp. 79-92.

Bandara, A. (2005): *Emerging Unemployment Issues in Asia and the Pacific: Rising to the Challenges*, UNESCAP.

Becattini, G. (1990), "The marshallian industrial district as a socio-economic notion", In: Pyke, F., Becattini, G. and Sengenberger. W. (Ed.) (1990): *Industrial Districts and Inter-Firm Cooperation in Italy*, International Institute for Labor Studies, Geneva, pp. 37-51.

Carroll, A.B. (1979): "A three-dimensional conceptual model of corporate performance", *Academy of Management Review*, Vol. 4, No. 4, pp. 497-505.

Chahoud, T., Emmerling, J., Kolb, D., Kubina, I., Repinski, G. and Schläger, C. (2007): *Corporate Social and Environmental Responsibility in India – Assessing the UN Global Compact's role*, German Development Institute, Bonn.

Chapple, W. and Moon, J. (2005): "Corporate social responsibility (CSR) in Asia: a seven-country study of CSR web site reporting", *Business & Society*, Vol. 44, No. 4, pp. 415-441.

Chopra, S. and Meindl, P. (2007): *Supply Chain Management*, Pearson, New Jersey.

CIA World Factbook (05/01/2010):
www.cia.gov/library/publications/the-world factbook/geos/in.html

Coase, R., (1937): "The nature of the firm", *Economica*, 4, 386-405.

Commission of the European communities (2001): "Green Paper - Promoting a European framework for corporate social responsibility", the commission, d. 18/7, Brussels

Cooper, M., Lampert, D. and Pagh, J. (1997): "Supply chain management: more than a new name for logistics", *International Journal of Logistics Management*, Vol. 8, No. 1, pp. 1-14.

Corbett, M.F., (2005): "Trends to watch 2005", *Fortune*, March 21, pp. B12.

CorpWatch Holding Corporations Accountable, found 20/12 2009, www.corpwatch.org
(http://www.corpwatch.org/article.php?list=class&type=189&class=3
&offset=25)

Corruption Perceptions Index 2009, found 20/12 2009, www.transparency.org
(transparency.org/policy_research/surveys_indices/cpi/2009/cpi_2009
_table)

Danish Ministry of Foreign Affairs (22/12/2009):
www.asien.um.dk/da/menu/InfoOmRegionen/LandefaktaAsien/Indien

Danish Minister for Economic and Business Affairs, Mrs Lene Espersen (2008), "Proposal for an Act amending the Danish Financial Statement Act (Report on social responsibility for large businesses)" www.eogs.dk (http://www.eogs.dk/graphics/Samfundsansvar.dk/Dokumenter/Prop osal_Report_On_Social_Resp.pdf)

De Langren, P.W. (2002): "Clustering and performance: the case of maritime clustering in the Netherlands", *Maritime Policy and Management*, Vol. 29, No. 3, pp. 209-221.

De Wit, B. and Meyer, R. (2004): *Strategy: Process, Content, Context*, International Thomson Business Press, London.

Doig, S., Ritter, R., Speckhals, K. and Woolson, D. (2001): "Has outsourcing gone too far?", *McKinsey Quarterly*, No. 4, pp. 25–37.

Dong-Hoon, Y., Seongcheol, K., Changi, N. and Ja-Won, M. (2007): "Developing a decision model for business process outsourcing", *Computers & Operations Research*, Vol. 34, No. 12, pp. 3769-3778.

Dunning, J.H. (1993): *"Multinational Enterprises and the Global Economy"*, Addison-Wesley, Reading.

Dunning, J.H. (1993): *Multinational Enterprises and the Global Economy*, Addison-Wesley, Reading.

Economy Watch (07/01/2010): www.economywatch.com/indianeconomy

Ellram, L., Tate, W. and Billington, C. (2008): "Offshore outsourcing of professional services: a transaction cost economics perspective", *Journal of Operations Management*, Vol. 26, No. 2, pp. 148–163.

EOGS (07/01/2010): www.eogs.dk

Etzkovitz, H. and Leydersdorff, L. (2000): "The dynamics of innovation: from national systems and "mode 2" to a triple helix of university – industry – government relations", *Research Policy*, Vol. 29, No. 2, pp. 109-123.

EU (2001), *Promoting a European framework for corporate social responsibility – Green Paper*, Brussel: Directory-General for Employment and Social Affairs, European Commission.

162

Flood, G.D. (1996): *An Introduction to Hinduism*, Cambridge University Press, Cambridge.

Fuller, C.J. (2004): *The Camphor Flame: Popular Hinduism and Society in Indian*, Princeton University Press, Princeton, New Jersey.

Frijs-Madsen, J. (2009): *Eksportfokus*, Eksportrådet, Udenrigsministeriet.

Frow, P. and Payne, A. (2009): "Customer relationships management: a strategic perspective, *Journal of Business Market Management*, Vol. 3, No. 1, pp. 7-27.

Fuller, C.J. (2004): *The Camphor Flame: Popular Hinduism and Society in India*, Princeton University Press, Princeton NJ.

Garner, B.A. (eds.) (2009): *Black's Law Dictionary*, Thomson Reuters, West Group.

Graf, M. and Mudambi, S. (2005): "The outsourcing of IT-enabled business processes: a conceptual model of the location decision", *Journal of International Management*, Vol. 11, No. 2, pp. 253-268.

Gruen, T.W. (1997): "Relationship marketing: the route to marketing efficiency and effectiveness", *Business Horizons*, Vol. 40, No. 6, pp. 32-38.

Government of Karnataka (2009): *Economic Survey 2008-09*, Government of Karnataka.

Government of India (05/01/2010): http://india.gov.in

Guenzi, P., Pardo, C. and Georges, L. (2007): "Relational selling strategy and key account managers' relational behaviors: an exploratory study", *Industrial Marketing Management*, Vol. 36, No. 1, pp. 121-133.

Heizer, J. and Render, B. (2009): *Operations Management*, Pearson Education International, New Jersey.

Heldbjerg, G. (2006): *Grøftegravning i metodisk perspektiv*, Samfundslitteratur, Gylling.

Hofstede, G. (1997): *Cultures and Organizations: Software of the Mind: Intercultural Cooperation and its Importance for Survival*, McGraw-Hill, New York.

Hofstede, G. (1980): *Culture's Consequences: International Differences in Work-Related Values*, Sage Publications, Beverly Hills, CA.

House, R.J., Hanges, P.J., Javidsen, M., Dorfman, P. and Gupta, V. (Eds.) (2004): *Culture, Leadership, and Organizations – The GLOBE Study of 62 Societies*, Sage Publications, Beverly Hills, CA.

Human Development Reports, found 20/12 2009, (http://hdr.undp.org/en/statistics/)

Hätönen, J. (2009): "Making the locational choice: a case approach to the development of a theory of offshore outsourcing and internationalization", *Journal of International Management*, Vol. 15, No. 1, pp. 61-76.

Ingstrup, M.B., Freytag, P.V. and Damgaard, T. (2009): "Cluster initiation and development: a critical view from a network perspective!", Competitive paper - submitted for the *IMP 2009 Conference at Euromed Management*, France.

Institut for menneskerettigheders Human Rights and Business Project i samarbejde med Dansk Industri og Økonomi- og Erhvervsministeriet (2007), "CSR kompasset, Landeprofil Indien", (http://www.csrkompasset.dk/DI/media/CRB_Indien.pdf)

International Organization for Standardization, found 20/12 2009, (http://www.iso.org/iso/about.htm)

Jobber, D. (2007): *Principles and Practice of Marketing*, McGraw-Hill Education, New York.

Jobber, D. and Lancaster, G. (2009): *Selling and Sales Management*, Prentice Hall, London.

Kjærsgaard, H. (2005): "Kastesystemet – hinduisme", Kristelig Dagblad, 25/5, Found 20/12 2009, (http://www.religion.dk/artikel/248514)

Kolk, A. and Pinkse, J. (2006), "Stakeholder mismanagement and corporate social responsibility crises", *European Management Journal*, Vol. 24, No. 1, pp. 59-72.

Lüthje, T. (2005): "Vertical specialization across developed countries", *International Trade Journal*, Vol. 19, No. 3, pp. 193-216.

Lynch, R. (1997), *Corporate Strategy*, Pitman Publishing, London.

Martin, R. and Sunley, P. (2003): "Deconstructing cluster: chaotic concept or policy panacea?", *Journal of Economic Geography*, Vol. 3, No. 1, pp. 5-35.

Marshall, A. (1930): *Principles of Economics*, Macmillan, London.

McKinsey, (2007): *The 'Bird of Gold': The Rise of India's Consumer Market*, McKinsey Global Institute

Mehta, A., Armenakis, A., Mehta, N. and Irani, F. (2006): "Challenges and opportunities of business process outsourcing in India", *Journal of Labor Research*, Vol. 27, No. 3, pp. 323-339.

Midttun, A., Gautesen, K. and Gjølberg, M. (2006): "The political economy of CSR in Western Europe", *Corporate Governance*, Vol. 6, No. 4, pp. 369-385.

Millman, T. and Wilson, K. (1995): "From key account selling to key account management", *Journal of Marketing Practice*, Vol. 1, No. 1, pp. 9-21.

Miltenburg, J. (2005): *Manufacturing Strategy*, Productivity Press, New York.

Monzka, R., Trent R., and Handfield, R. (1998): *Purchasing and Supply Chain Management*, South-Western College Publishing, Mason, OH.

OECD (2008): *OECD Economic Outlook 83 – Chapter 2: Developments in Individual OECD Countries and Selected Non-member Economies*, OECD. Organization for Economic Co-Operation and Development, found 20/12 2009,(http://www.oecd.org/about/0,3347,en_2649_34859_1_1_1_1_1, 00.html)

Pagadala, P.M., and Mulaik, S. (2009): "Why you should be in India now", *Supply Chain Quarterly*, quarter 1, 2009, pp. 28-33.

P.A.P – Blog Human Rights etc., Human Rights Facts (54): The Indian Caste System, 19/8 2008, found 20/12 2009, (http://filipspagnoli.wordpress.com/2008/08/19/human-rights-facts-54-the-indian-caste-system/)

Porter, M.E. (2008): *On Competition – Updated and Expanded Edition*, Harvard Business School Publishing, Boston.

Prieto-Carrón, M., Lund-Thomsen, P., Chan, A., Muro, A. and Bhushan, C. (2006): "Critical perspectives on CSR and development: what we know, what we don't know, and what we need to know", *International Affairs*, Vol. 82, No. 5, pp. 977-987

Pyndt, J. and Pedersen, T. (2006): *Managing Global Offshoring Strategies: A Case Approach*, Copenhagen Business School Press, Gylling.

Ramachandran, K. and Voleti, S. (2004): "Business process outsourcing (BPO): emerging scenario and strategic options for IT-enabled services", *Vikalpa*, Vol. 29, No. 1, pp. 49-63.

Roy, T. (2007): "Globalization, factor prices, and poverty in colonial India", *Australian Economic History Review*, Vol. 47, No. 1, pp. 73-94.

Rushton, A. and Walker, S. (2007): *International Logistics and Supply Chain Outsourcing – From Local to Global*, The Chartered institute of Logistics and Transport (UK).

Sagar, P and Singla, A. (2004): "Trust and corporate social responsibility: Lessons from India", *Journal of Communication Management*, Vol. 8, No. 3, pp. 282-290.

Schein, E.H. (1984), "Coming to a new awareness of organizational culture", *Sloan Management Review*, Vol. 25, No. 2, pp. 3-16.

Shiralashetti, A.S., and Hugar, S.S. (2009): "Foreign direct investment and economic development of India: a diagnostic study", *The Icfai University Journal of Managerial Economics*, Vol. 7, No. 1, pp. 54-69.

Sivananda, S. (1999): *All About Hinduism: A Divine Life Society Publication*, http://www.dlshq.org/download/hinduismbk.htm

Storper, M. (1995): "The resurgence of regional economies, ten years later: the region as a nexus of untraded Interdependencies", *European Urban and Regional Studies*, Vol. 2, No. 3, pp. 191-222.

Tamil Nadu Online (22/12-2009): www.tamilnaduonline.in/Profile/Economy.

The Hindu (22/12-2009):
www.hindu.com/2005/04/22/stories/2005042211030100.htm.

Thorat, S. (2002): "Oppression and denial: dalit discrimination in the 1990s", *Economic and Political Weekly*, Vol. 37, No. 6, pp. 572-578.

UNCTAD (2009): *World Investment Report 2009: Transnational Corporations, Agricultural Production and Development*, United Nations.

United Nations Global Compact, found 20/12 2009, (http://www.unglobalcompact.org/AboutTheGC/TheTenPrinciples/index.html)

van Liempd, D. (2007): *An Introduction to Corporate Social Responsibility*, Department of Entrepreneurship and Relationship Management, University of Southern Denmark.

Welford, R. (2005): *Corporate Social Responsibility in Europe, North America and Asia, 2004 Survey Results*, Greenleaf Publishing, University of Hong Kong, China.

Wengler, S., Ehret, M. and Saab, S. (2006): "Implementation of key account management: who, why and how? an exploratory study on the current implementation of key account management programs", *Industrial Marketing Management*, Vol. 35, No. 1, pp. 103-112.

Williamson, O. (1981): "The economics of organization: the transaction cost approach", *American Journal of Sociology*, Vol. 87, No. 3, pp. 548-577.

Worldwide Legal Directories, found 20/12 2009, (http://www.hg.org/lawfirms/Bribery/India.html)

# Index

A Cooperative Relationships Model; 109

Back-Office Activities; 54
Back-office processing; 35
Bangalore; 27
Brains of the world; 31
Bribery; 145
Building a Relationship; 115
Business Process Outsourcing; 34

Case by Case Participant; 88
Caste System; 129
Cheminova A/S; 15
Chennai; 27
Cluster Location Matrix; 86
Clusters; 63
Competence-Based Perspective; 40
Competitive Cluster; 67
Corporate Social Responsibility; 121
Corruption Perceptions Index; 146
CSR Paradoxes; 127
CSR, defined; 125
CSR-policy; 139
Cultural dimensions; 105

Danfoss Industries Pvt Ltd; 15
Danish Financial Statement Act; 138
Democracy; 111
Domestic outsourcing; 37
Embedded strategy approach; 133
Enthusiastic Participant; 88
Environmental factors; 97
Fabrikant Mads Clausens Fond; 15

Factors Affecting BPO Decision; 42
FLSmidth; 16
Front-Office Activities; 53
Front-office processing, ;35

Global CSR-strategy; 136
Global Recession; 111
GLOBE Framework; 96
Grundfos; 16

Indian Culture; 96
Indian population; 22
ISO; 137

Karma; 128
Karnataka; 27
Key Account Management; 115
Key Account Management Process; 101

Languages in India; 23
Local CSR-strategy; 136
Location Attractiveness; 45
Location decision; 43
Location specific advantages; 75
Locational Competitive Advantage; 72
Lundbeck; 15

Make-or-Buy; 37
Middle-Office Activities; 53
Middle-office processing; 35
Minimum labor requirements; 143
Modern India; 122
Most giving cultural learning; 156
Most impressive experiences; 152

Motives for Responsible Conduct; 126

NGO; 141
Non-Governmental Organization; 12
Novozymes; 15

OECD; 145
Off-shore outsourcing; 37
Off-shoring; 35
Off-shoring strategy; 62
Ole Kirks Fond; 15
OLI framework; 43
Outside agencies employees; 142
Outsourcing; 34
Outsourcing strategy; 62
Own workforce; 142

PESTEL; 97
Philanthropic approach; 133
Piapium; 16
Porter's Cluster Theory; 72
Purpose of the course; 151

Relational Strategies; 102
Relational View; 41
Relationship Management; 93
Religion in India; 24
Reluctant Participant; 88

Samrat Gems Impex PVT. Ltd; 15
Santa Fe; 15
Strategic Driver; 88

Tamil Nadu; 27
The Varna system; 130
Toosbuys Fond; 15
Trade Commission of Denmark; 15
Transaction-Cost Theory; 39
Triple Helix; 63

UN Global Compact; 126
UNGC; 137
UST Global; 16

Valcon; 16
Vestas; 16

# About the Editors

*Jan Stentoft Arlbjørn*, Ph.D., is a Professor in Supply Chain Management (SCM) at the Department of Entrepreneurship and Relationship Management, University of Southern Denmark, Kolding. His research and teaching areas are within SCM, Supply Chain Innovation, Enterprise Resource Planning, and Corporate Social Responsibility. He has practical industry experience from positions as Director (Programme Management Office) at LEGO Systems A/S, Axapta ERP Project Manager at Gumlink A/S, and as management consultant in a wide number of industrial enterprises from his own consulting practice.

*Henning de Haas,* Ph.D. is a Post Doc in Supply Chain Management (SCM) at the Department of Entrepreneurship and Relationship Management, University of Southern Denmark, Kolding. His research and teaching areas are within SCM, Supply Chain Innovation, Operations Management, and Sustainable Supply Chain Management. He has practical industry experience in leading and managing supply chain optimization in different companies like Bang & Olufsen A/S, LEGO System A/S and BB Electronics A/S, and as management consultant in a wide number of industrial enterprises from his own consulting practice.

*Dennis van Liempd,* Ph.D., is an Assistant Professor in Accounting and Auditing at the Department of Entrepreneurship and Relationship Management, University of Southern Denmark, Kolding. His research and teaching areas include amongst others Corporate Social Responsibility and Sustainability (also in an SCM context), CSR reporting, and CSR auditing. He holds master degrees in business economics from Radboud University, Nijmegen, Holland, and from University of Southern Denmark, Kolding, and has studied at the Carlson School of Management, University of Minnesota, Minneapolis, USA. He has furthermore worked as an Honorary Research Associate at Monash University, Melbourne, Australia.

*Mads Bruun Ingstrup* is a Ph.D. student in cluster development and economic geography at the Department of Entrepreneurship and Relationship Management, University of Southern Denmark, Kolding. His research and teaching areas are within off-shoring, outsourcing, cluster development, cluster facilitation, cluster policy, regional innovation systems and network strategy. He holds a master degree in international business development and has completed university studies at the Vienna University of Economics and Business Administration, Austria and at the Helsinki School of Economics, Finland.